SERENDIPITY
On Angel Wings

BETTY LOWREY

ISBN 979-8-9906818-1-1 (paperback)
ISBN 979-8-9906818-0-4 (eBook)

Printed in the United States of America

For Ruth and John

We are never so lost that
Angels can't find us

Unknown

Chapter One

Caught between a wish and a worry, that's what it was. She was no school girl, for Heaven's sakes. Still, she relived their telephone conversation. "I'm coming to see you, my lady. I have the information entered into my GPS. I will see you soon." What did it matter that he was in the states? Helplessly, she wondered and worried telling herself it didn't, but it did. Why was he coming here? Couldn't he have called and said they could meet in one of the distant-not-too-close towns? She walked the floor, then outside and found herself on that familiar path she and Wade had followed to their secret and special place. The bench was there and beneath it stamped in the concrete their message.

She sank onto the bench, wringing her hands in her lap, her hair falling around her face. If anyone looked they wouldn't see the despair written there. She had made her own bed, so to speak, and now must lie in it. Oh, Lord, she whispered, please make this town invisible, or put up a road block, whatever it takes to keep my neighbors from knowing my transgressions. If it be your will, let him call and I'll meet him wherever you think is safe from prying eyes. That said, she returned home, picked up the keys and got into the car.

Her next stop was the cemetery. The granite of Wade's stone was cool beneath the touch of her hand. The words seemed to scream *traitor*; Wade Allen Norman born, died, the dates etched in her mind, and blurred her vision. She wanted to fall to her knees, perhaps prostrate herself beneath the stone. Where are you? Her heart cried out, but she knew he wasn't there. All those months of suffering, because neither of them would turn loose, and he suffered until they saw no future and she realized he was more into leaving than staying. Who wanted to live life in a body wracked with pain wasting away?

Straightening, she placed both hands on top of the stone, Lord, give me good thoughts. Take this pain and sorrow from me, else let me die. I can stand no more. Have you removed your love from me, Lord? *"Ask and it shall be given you, seek and you will find; knock and it shall be given unto you." Matthew 7:7* The words filed through her mind. *"You ask for someone to talk to, Suze, and I granted your wish. Now you want me to block that person's entry into your life. You made the decision. Not me."*

Suze looked up to heaven. Was the Lord speaking to her or was she imagining things? *"Good thoughts, Suze? Remember how you and Wade met? You were on your way home from school. You saw the playground swing. Glancing around to be certain no one saw you, you were pumping away, enjoying flying through the air, when you heard him laugh. Wade was the one who found you. You thought he would make fun of you, but he didn't. He took the other swing. That was your first time together."*

"It was good," Suze whispered. "We laughed and talked and he said he always wanted to try out the swings but smaller children were usually present and he hadn't taken the chance, besides he didn't want the guys his age laughing at him. He was on the basketball team; he didn't need anyone teasing him. We understood each other."

"What else?"

Suze glanced around to see if in fact someone was near and playing tricks on her, but she was alone. "We began to date. Wade was courteous and attentive. He was a good friend. *"There's more."* Suze grinned. "Yes, he gave me his class ring, we went to Prom together and two years later we were married." Suze took a deep breath. *"But it wasn't enough was it, Suze, even though Wade was ill?"*

"It was enough, to be happy, but why did you take him? You are the great physician. You could have healed him." A span of silence made her think she had angered God, if that was who was talking to her. *"I am Alpha and Omega, Suze, the beginning and the end, for you there will be a great mystery. You are not to know everything. Your job is to trust me. Try trusting me from now on."* Proverbs 3:5-6 *Trust in the Lord with all your heart and lean not on your own understanding, in all your ways acknowledges Him and He shall direct your paths.*

She waited. There were no other words. She drove home, wondering if she had finally lost her mind, but she could not believe if that were true she would have received scripture that even now was alive, word by word, and remembered. But what was she to do about the gentleman intending to visit her?

"I can't make deals, Lord. I don't have anything to offer. It's better if he didn't come to New Haven."

The light on the message machine was blinking. Suze crossed the room and pushed a button. His voice began, "For some strange reason, Suze, I'm thinking you would prefer to meet away from your community. I've made arrangements to stay in the Cape, if that meets your approval, please reply. I send my love to you on angel's wings." Suze began to laugh. This was not by coincidence. "If you are able to meet me at the Garden Room…" She jotted down the time, place and date. For the first time in weeks she felt relief. She looked up. *Thank you.*

The phone rang again. Suspicious, Suze viewed the name. "Mabel?"

"Yes, where have you been? We are supposed to meet with the Sewing Group this afternoon."

"No worry, Mabel, I'll be there." Hurriedly she spread peanut butter on a slice of bread, picked up her keys and left the house. "I pray there will be no conflict and if there is, please send Hannah home." She walked the parking lot, noticing the designer's van was in the lot. The people had been satisfied with her work when the Sanctuary suffered from the fire that began with the small heater in the baptistery and now they called her back when they were unsure what to do with items needing refurbishing.

A new oil painting was being hung in the foyer where the previous was either stolen or damaged and hidden away. Now and then the people discussed the mystery of the painting not resurfacing in the community, but no one had seen it. For a moment, Suze considered the woman believed to have the oil, but then no one was certain and the matter was hushed. After all, Miss Britany James was a wealthy contributor to Shining Light Church. Miss Britany could probably buy any number of oils. Suze tried to make up for her own meager contribution by giving of her time whenever need arose.

"My, you look good today," Mabel met her at the door, carrying an unopened box of material suitable for the pads the women were known to make and distribute to the neighboring towns and New Haven's Nursing home. Mabel was scrutinizing, Suze. "What's different? Did you win the lottery?"

Suze shook her head. "Stop it." Now they were entering the room, to the buzz of busy machines.

"Well, it's been a long time coming, your paleness receding and a few extra pounds on your frame." Mabel set the box on a long table, found a knife in the drawer beneath, and slit open the top. "Truly, my friend, I have worried over you since Wade died. You have mourned a long time."

* * * * *

Marigold heard the whir and grind of machines. By now she knew Shining Light's schedule. Ruthie was in school and she had come alone to hang the painting Matt had done to replace the one that had been either destroyed or stolen. The new one was not the Woman at the Well; Matt had felt the need to paint the good shepherd standing in the midst of his sheep. Jesus mantle over his robe was a deep satisfying red. She could not forget the pleasure of viewing the Woman at the Well and how the colors seemed to draw one in. Matt had contributed his paintings and Harriet had paid the expense of refinishing the Sanctuary. Everything was beautiful. Marigold sighed. While her own shop was floundering she could not safely justify making contributions other than her own time and talent.

She promised Ruthie she would check on Pastor Merkel's wife. Leah and Ruthie had formed an unusual friendship. Leah once remarked Ruthie's visit always left her feeling settled and blessed in the spirit. Gathering up the tools, she placed them in a heavy tapestry bag and sit it by the door. She would take the short cut through the concourse, follow the path from the church to the Pastor's home and hopefully find Leah, although most of the women of Shining Light's congregation were in the sewing room, but she hadn't seen Leah. A sharp knock on the door and Leah appeared.

"Marigold, come in here, you look like you are ready to pop. Should you be traveling alone? Your little mate and my little friend is back in school, isn't she?" The two hugged. Leah motioned for Marigold to follow, leading to two chairs, but Marigold was standing observing her host. "What?" Leah questioned. "Is something wrong?"

"I haven't seen you since the Praise Festival. There's something different about you. Are…you…" She hesitated. "Something's going on and Ruthie hasn't told me." Marigold began to laugh."That little stinker. You're pregnant aren't you?" Leah was nodding, proudly. "And let me guess, the baby is due somewhere around April, am I right?"

"How would you know that? And you…oh, girl, you definitely should not be traveling this distance alone." Leah reached for a pillow, "here, sit beside me, so we can talk."

"You know Ruthie, once asked me when tulips bloomed and I had a distinct feeling the timing concerned you and all I could think was, you were pregnant or either Ruthie was working out one of those insights she receives. Call it revelations, if you wish. Is she close on the time?"

Leah grinned,"Close, unless we run into problems."

"Well, there are those late blooming tulips. Harriet has a string that lasts March through May." Carefully, Marigold slid onto the sofa, letting her body ease into the soft upholstery. "I probably shouldn't have come alone, but sometimes you do what you must and it's done now."

"What was your mission this time?"

"Replacing the lost oil." Marigold freed her feet from shoes. "Don't guess anyone has located it?"

Briefly a frown crossed Leah's brow. "You know Britany James has been staying with Mabel Hisaw," she nodded as Marigold's eyes grew large. "Yes, she is still here, recovering from a near mental break down, according to what the doctor told Mabel. You know in losing her parents, unable to convince your husband he should divorce you and marry her. I know…it's pitiful. We are all a bit leery of Britany."

"I will never forget seeing Britany lying in the street under the table that day of the shooting, when the man we thought was Herm Smith turned out to be his cousin, Walden. Herm was actually tied up out in the country and probably would have died if Ruthie hadn't had one of her visions." Marigold sighed. "But Britany wasn't hit by the stray bullet, for some reason she had passed out… someone said drug overdose of prescription drugs, which Walden had been giving her to help her deal with depression."

"What is that old saying, *Oh, the web we weave when first we practice to deceive*? I don't know which one was worse, Walden or Britany James…and then there was Herm, who really did have a mental problem, Walden, being his own cousin, was feeding him some kind of drug that nearly robbed Herm of his sanity. Some kind of mind altering drug Walden had been hiding all those months, but also dipping into it himself." Leah closed her eyes, thinking. "It's taken months to unravel the story and as I understand to clear your friend in the Cape. Is he back with his family now?"

"Andrew is with his family, finally, but he lost the opportunity for a better job with an outstanding group in the Cape. When they thought he had killed someone, of course they withdrew the offer and hired someone else." Leaning toward Leah, Marigold questioned, "How did Pastor handle the oddity of having two in his congregation that were major participants with Walden in the drug bust?"

"We had so much going on; I think it all had to play out in its own time. Of course, that's when we found out I was pregnant." A happy smile crossed Leah's face. "Seven years of hoping and giving up and then God blesses us." Tears brightened her eyes. "We almost ended our marriage and then to find out we were expecting a baby."

"I'm happy for you." Marigold glanced at the large gold faced watch on her wrist. "Oh, I've got to go."

"But you just got here." Leah watched Marigold struggle to stand, rising herself without effort.

"Matt is still overseeing his parent's farm and he is meeting me at the shop. Then I'll head home."

"Where's your little boy?" Leah placed a hand on Marigold's. "Anytime you would like to bring him, you can leave him with me while you do your work. I'd love to sit with him and learn a thing or two."

"You would learn something." Marigold grinned. "M.J. is the love of our life. It is difficult his daddy being away helping with the farm and us in the Cape, but if Matt's father recovers that will end."

"He will return when the baby is due?" Leah watched Marigold trying to slip swollen feet into shoes.

"That's for certain, but harvest should be ended and Matt will be home. He wants to be home with us."

"I understand Matt's mother is hard to deal with? Has anything changed?" Leah saw the sadness in Marigold's eyes. "I'm so sorry. Levi's mother is a saint, but she has her own struggle in the Nursing Unit."

"Sadly, Vivien Langley wants Britany James to be her daughter in law but happily her son wants me."

Leah reached over to give Marigold a hug. "I'll pray that changes and Britany comes to her senses, too."

"It will take a miracle for Britany James to give up Matt, but Vivien encourages her every step."

Chapter Two

Matt throttled down, allowing the tractor to come to a stop. His face wreathed in smile as he bound down the ladder. This was his bride come to meet him, the love of his life. Some days he thought he could not bear another day away from Marigold and M.J., but the demands of the farm were many. She was slow to climb from the van. Immediately his eyes were drawn to her feet. They were swollen but more importantly he noticed she was wearing flats. When his beloved gave up heels for flats he knew there was a problem. Something inside quickened and he felt the old worry, remembering when M.J. was born.

His arms went around her; her head was on his shoulder. He loved the way she melt into his body. Her arms circled his neck as he kissed her once, drew back to look into her eyes and kissed her again. "What's going on, Tinkerbell?" With one finger beneath her chin, he tilt her head to study her features. Her eyes were half-closed; she seemed more fatigued than he remembered. The passion he'd felt seeing her, changed to a depth of caring so deep it scared him. Marigold had almost died having M.J.

"Babe?"

"I'm just tired and having your arms around me lets me relax." She sighed, shaking her head, "Without you, I run a tense race, pushing all day long…sometimes I think, pushing just to get through that day."

"Aw, Babe, that's not good. Not with it almost time to deliver the baby."

"I'll be all right."

"Come on, get in the back of the van, I'll sit with you." He helped her in, closed the door and walked to the other side. "How long have you been this way? Tired, or whatever it is?" Settling into the leather seat, he leaned in to hear her reply. At the moment, his heart was in his stomach, she looked frail.

"I hung the last oil you did for the church. It looks good but maybe not as rich as the woman at the well." She gave a tired laugh. "If you gave up farming for painting you would be home with me and M.J."

"We'd all be skinny, too. Somehow I doubt I could feed my growing boy on my talent."

"I dunno. There's a letter laying on the mantel, a church in Indiana saw your work at the gallery and want to commission you to do a painting. They sent a check to encourage you."

"Really?" A smile broke across his face. "How much?"

"You," she wagged a finger, "will have to come home to see."

"The Lord knows I'm ready." For a moment he wished he could ride home with Marigold, have no burden on his heart to oversee the crop coming out of the field on his father's farm. He sighed so deeply, Marigold reached for his hand. He swallowed down the lump in his throat, glancing to Marigold. "I don't suppose you have any idea?"

"About you coming home?" She settled farther down into the seat. "Can you go tonight?"

Their time together was so short it seemed to have only begun when she leaned down trying to slip her feet back into the flats. "Babe," worry and shock flooded his mind, while she had sit talking with him, her feet had practically doubled in size. He was trying to help her but the shoe would not go on. "Marigold, what is wrong. We can't get your shoes on those feet and you've miles to travel."

"It's a common thing. I'm used to it."

"Well, I'm not." His eyes were troubled and his heart ached. "I am so torn. I think I'm in the wrong place." He ran a hand over his forehead, staring at the ground, as his lips quivered. "I'm ashamed. I feel this need to help dad get the crop out of the fields and here you are…" He was standing outside the opened door as she was trying to climb out of the back seat and he didn't know how to help her. He stretched out a hand; she took it until finally her feet touched the ground. "Lord help us." He pulled her into his arms. "Babe, I'll make it up to you."

She was so tired all she could manage was to pat Matt on the back, as his tears ran down her cheek. "It's all right, Farm Boy. I know you love me." She sighed. "I'm too tired to cry, I've found it only wears me out quicker so I try not to anymore. Lonely nights, I just pull M.J. closer."

He gave a muffled groan, part cry, part laughter, "I pummel the pillow at Nate's until I think the stuffing will fly."

"How is Nate?" Matt was helping her into the driver's seat. She saw his concern and tried to lighten the matter. "Leah told me Britany is living with Mrs. Hisaw. I wondered about that, but I didn't pry."

"Yeah," Matt leaned on the window post. "Nate tells me Walden had been giving both Britany and Smith some kind of drug, mind altering, whatever that means. You know he was the one stole all the drugs from the Cartel and they came after him but didn't find anything but they left since the law was on them."

"I still don't understand Britany's connection to Walden or Herm Smith or her living at Mrs. Hisaw's.

Matt grinned. "Do you want me to find out?" He saw a fiery glint dart through her eyes and hurried to lay his forehead against hers. Nose to nose, he tried to soften her feelings, "You know I don't go around her, Tinkerbell. Sometimes, I feel we are dating again…I don't get to see you or hold you." His voice turned serious. "Will you be all right driving home?" He was kissing her. "Don't answer, this is better."

She left with a bit more adrenalin flowing through her veins than when she arrived. Her thoughts were on the strange connection between Britany James and Walden and where was the elusive Walden? She shuddered, remembering it was Harriet's maid; Hattie, the hero, the day Walden found his way to Anne at Harriet's home. He expected Anne to help him retrieve the case of stolen drugs hidden beneath Andrew and Anne's home. For some strange reason, providential, for certain, Hattie had knocked Walden out with an iron skillet. He had torn her apron straps off in the process but Hattie was victor.

Daniel Gates told the story of the children marching along with Harriet, "Little soldiers," he would say as his countenance took on a faraway look and he shook his head, "I'm telling you, God was watching over them, Walden was so deranged he would have shot them on the spot and thought nothing of it."

She knew God was watching over her family, but the separation was killing her. Maybe she had given up crying tears but her heartache the first hours of the night meant she wasn't sleeping well and the doctor kept impressing on her that rest was of great importance to her and the baby.

She arrived back in the Cape as the evening shadows were drawing down, thankful to see the shop was closed and passed it on by to pick up M.J. from Harriet's. Leaving supplies in the van, she pocketed the keys, straightened her clothes and walked bare foot into the house. The serenity of her birth mother's home was always striking. Quality furnishings were one thing, but the atmosphere Harriet was able to portray brought calm to a weary soul. There were times she wanted to settle into the overstuffed chairs where she and Harriet sit in front of the windows and soak up the peace she always felt as in the winter months rays of sunshine touched the room, but now the air felt good and with aching feet she sank down with a slight groan of appreciation and closed her eyes for a moment before collecting her son.

Harriet stood in the doorway. The pregnancy was full blown, Marigold's body swollen. *My child. My child.* She saw the gray beneath Marigold's eyes. When her glance came to Marigold's feet, she pinched her lips tight lest a gasp escape. What was going on here? She stepped closer, bending to see, bare feet, the skin tight and shiny. There was a problem and Marigold was asleep. She sank in the chair opposite her daughter, her mind whirring in a thousand directions. Marigold would be angry if she called a doctor, but then there was Dr. Silverstone on the corner. It was not unusual to find them together playing cards. He was a good friend. She tiptoed to the kitchen, made the call and told him not to knock but to come in and sit where he could observe her daughter.

His expression grim, Dr. Silverstone motioned to Harriet they should return to the kitchen. "Has Marigold had any history of heart problems?"

"You think it's her heart?" Harriet almost hissed, anxiety covering the need to be quiet. "No. But she had a hard delivery with M.J. She almost died delivering him." She stood staring at him. "Why would you think her heart?"

"I'm a heart surgeon, Harriet, not an obstetrician, but Marigold is swollen, not only her feet but her body." He shook his head. "She needs to see her doctor as soon as possible."

They were hesitant to waken her; finally deciding to take the chance she wouldn't stir they elevated her feet onto a foot stool, and then tiptoed from the room. Dr. Silverstone left saying his doctor friends would arrive any moment for a card game. Harriet checked on M.J. playing with Andrew under Anne's watchful eye and returned to the kitchen where she picked up the phone and made a call.

Hearing the hall clock strike eight, Marigold listened for sounds of M.J. playing, a flood of adrenalin coursing her veins as she realized she was still sitting in Harriet's chair by the window in Harriet's home. What had she done, fallen asleep while having conversation with her mother? Then it came to her, they hadn't even spoken. She started to rise when Harriet came into the room, holding M.J.'s hand.

"Look at our young man, all scrubbed clean from the sand box, fed and ready to see his Momma." Harriet beamed as she pulled a second stool closer for M.J. to climb on to. "How are you feeling, now that you've rested," She asked. The smile dimmed at her daughter's hesitance but she covered quickly. She was thankful M.

J. was talking over her in his excited rehearsal of the day's activities, the ice cream truck his favorite time.

"It's got a bell, Momma. Nana says it's to tell all the little boys and girls he's on his way and we could hear it down the block, all the way to Mr. Shumacher's store. We know that because we went out and waited for it."

Marigold was pulling him onto her lap, finding there really wasn't enough room for him to sit. Her eyes met Harriet's. "This baby inside won't let my boy sit on my lap tonight. It feels like baby gained ten pounds today." She leaned to kiss M.J.'s forehead as he slid back onto the stool. He was patting what there was of her lap.

"It's okay, Momma, I'm big I can sit here. You want to eat, Momma? Nana's got some really good cookies, but you have to eat your vegetables first. Don't she, Nana?"

Stooping down to his level, Harriet smiled and kissed his cheek. "Have I told you, you have been the best boy ever, today?" She turned to Marigold. "Andy was here, too and they played something fierce. At two I told them they had to take a nap and they did. Now how many grammas have that?"

"Gramma, is it?" There was teasing in Marigold's tone. "Wouldn't Farm Boy laugh hearing that?"

Harriet stretched out a hand. "Come on, Hattie left you a plate"

"Hattie stayed that late?"

"She can hardly bear to leave these boys. When Anne left with Andy I sent her on her way, too."

"Maybe I'll see her next time." Yawning, Marigold followed. "You are about the best Momma, ever," she teased, reaching to lay an arm around Harriet's shoulders. "I don't know what I'd without you."

"It wasn't always that way," Harriet gave her a reckoning eye. "Once I thought it might never happen."

"Well," Marigold hugged her to her body. "You didn't like my decorations, as I recall, said they were too garish, and looked like Halloween instead of Thanksgiving. Now that hurt."

"Shush." Glancing up, Harriet asked, "Were your adoptive parents tall?"

Marigold slid onto the bar stool, taking in Harriet's stature, "Not really tall. Dad was six feet, I guess and Mom about my height, I thought you were six feet when we were doing all our insults to each other, but tonight you seem to have shrunk, I have no problem whatsoever laying my arm around your shoulders. Why?" She was lifting the glass dome from the plate. "Wow, a full five coarse meal. Who has that?" The first fork full was disappearing. "Oh, my goodness,

Hattie cooks like an angel. Anyway, so I'm a bit taller than you, why did you mention my adoptive parents?"

"Because, your birth father was a tall man, I'd say six four." Harriet sighed. "I hadn't thought of him in years."

The fork paused, mid-air. "Can I meet him?" She lay the fork down on the counter. "I never thought of it before." Marigold stared down at the plate, and then raised her eyes to meet Harriet's. "Now as inquisitive as I am, why wouldn't I have demanded to meet him? I think maybe I thought you didn't want me to…"

"I probably shied away from the subject, and our lives have been full, maybe we decided to be thankful for what we have, once we came to our senses." Harriet wished she had never voiced a word on height.

"So, do you know where he is? Can I meet him?" Marigold leaned toward Harriet. "What kind of man was he? Is he now?"

A rush of blood brought warmth to Harriet's face. "He was a scoundrel. I would have given him the world if I could, but he lied to me, led me on and then deserted me." Harriet stood there staring into space, her shoulders drawn forward, and a miserable expression on her face. Marigold slid off the stool and came to Harriet, her arms encircling her mother. Tears were falling, unbidden from Harriet. Bringing her hands to hide the tears, she could not look at Marigold. Harriet's concern wasn't for him; it was the state her child's feet were in.

"Ma," using Matt's word of endearment for Harriet, Marigold rocked her, in her arms, not letting go. "It's all right. You've held this in all those years." Rocking, slowly, then to a standstill, Marigold led her mother to the sitting room. M.J. had trailed off to the playroom and they heard the clicking of wooden building blocks. "Now, let's talk. Where is my birth father?"

"He died." Harriet choked on her own words. "When he told me how foolish I was to think he would be a father to my child, that

I should have an abortion and go somewhere and rebuild my life, that he was not part of, he had all the children he could care for, I never saw him again. I had nothing but I was determined to give my baby a good start. I went to this home in Texas that cared for unwed girls who came there, not knowing what the future held but usually giving their child up for adoption and they found this lovely couple who could not have a child…I was allowed to hold you and then you were placed in their arms and twenty years later you found me." Fresh tears fell between them.

"Ma, look at me." Marigold waited. "You have such composure and the presence of a military general. I never knew you still hurt over this…and I'm sorry you had such sadness, but Ma, you gave me life and I'm grateful." Her own voice wavered. "That meant I was found by Matt and allowed to birth M.J." Her heart was racing with the knowledge of being blessed so much more than she gave credit. "Oh, Ma, I love you." She reached for Harriet again. "Who knew it would take this long for me to realize what I have?"

Chapter Three

Newhaven

Although she wasn't expecting him, Nate drove over to see Mabel. He knocked. She came to the door, wearing some kind of strange cap on her head. Embarrassed, she gave him a strange look and invited him in. It was a moment before a slight grin began forming on Nate's face and she chuckled, eyebrows raised as he studied her strange garb. Arms outstretched, she turned a slow circle in front of him.

"So, I'll warn you, this is what a woman wears when she's ridding the back porch of spider webs and bugs. I don't know why but they are bad and somehow they have come inside." She was removing the cap, and unbuttoning a faded duster to stand before him fully dressed, the tidy, strapping woman he remembered. "There, is that better?" She rolled the two pieces together. "Come with me."

He followed. "You know, Mabel, there's never a dull moment with you. A man never knows what to expect." He chuckled as she pointed to the small pan on the floor, filled with worms and a few wads of what he supposed were spider webs that usually formed in the corners of rooms. "It looks as though you have an army worm infestation. Has anyone sprayed?" She was shaking her head, picking up the pan, staring at the contents. "Any moving," he asked.

"No. They're goners but those on the bushes out back are thriving."

"You have a sprayer, Mabel?"

"Yes, that I do, but I don't know what to use on them." She frowned, thinking a moment. "Aren't they late?"

"We've had unseasonably warm weather, after that rainy spell, such things off-set nature." He turned back. "If you know where your sprayer is, I'll run to the hardware, get the spray and do this job for you."

Mabel started to protest but he was already out the front door headed toward his truck. He was headed toward town when he remembered; his whole point in the visit was to check on Britany, not that it wasn't always nice to see Mabel. For a moment memory, of them a twosome in youth, surfaced. She was just as pleasant to be with now as then, but he reminded himself there was a lot of water under the bridge.

Thirty minutes later he was spraying the bushes and wondering about Suze's property. "Why don't you call Suze," he said. "There's enough spray left if she has need and I'll go down there and take care of it."

It was later, when Mabel asked them both to stay for lunch. "It's the old fashioned kind, with Britany spending a few days away I decided it was a good time for an all-out beans and potato dinner with cabbage and corn bread. Don't you worry, Nate, there's ham in the beans to fill a man's meat appetite."

"What do you mean, Britany's away?" A slash of worry raced through Nate. "Is she up to going off by herself?"

"You mean she didn't drop by to see you before she left." Mabel was cutting the cornbread into slices. "She definitely said she would see you. But then, young folks change their minds, don't they?"

"In this case, do you think the doctor felt it wise for her to strike out on her own?"

Mabel sit down across from Nate, reaching for Suze hand as they prepared to say grace. "I don't know, Nate. Why don't you say grace over our food and together we'll remember Britany's needs wherever she is."

The conversation was lively and the laughter lift their spirits. Nate and Mabel relived a portion of their courtship for Suze, omitting Vivien Langley in the telling, but touching briefly on Britany's fixation on Matt. "I declare," Nate said, "Matt's the best young fellow I've ever met, bar none, and much as I love Britany, mind you if he weren't married I might wish she'd win him over, but truth is, Britany's spoiled and Matt's too good a man to have to deal with her wants."

When the conversation dulled, Suze felt it time to go home. "I'll help with the dishes," she said, rising.

"That's my job," Nate replied. "It's been many a year since me and Mabel cleared a table. Maybe we need to revive those skills." He grinned. "Tomorrow, when we drive through the fields, we'll stop off and have a bite at my house. That housekeeper," he shook his head, his expression changing, "She's different, all right, nearly scared Matt out of his wits, but she's a fine cook. Like you, Mabel."

Suze was aware of Mabel's sudden shyness. There was that look going between the two again. They wouldn't know if she ducked out the door. She heard Nate's goodbye as she closed the screen gently behind her. She had wanted to tell them she would be out of town, but lately, bravery wasn't her cup of tea. Maybe they wouldn't even miss her. Come Sunday she would be back in her usual pew. With the two of them keeping company, she just might pull this off without anyone knowing after all.

At home, she found the overnight case in the back of the closet and ran her hand across the damask covering with its fine silken strings. She had few occasions to use Wade's gift; shades of teal, a bit of soft yellow and green meld together in the raised cover design. It brought her great comfort remembering the day Wade had given it to her. "Now we can go into town in style, Mrs. Norman. Throw away that old cracked leather weekender from high school days. Honey, you are vogue. Um, Humm!" He had twirled her around the room, both of them falling at last onto the four poster bed.

A moment of despair claimed her. What was she doing? A feeling of guilt coursed her veins. It always surfaced when her secret companion ended his mail to her. Why did he say he sent his love on angel wings? He didn't know her. Wade, her heart cried out, but he was gone. It had come to this, she was to meet this stranger she felt she already knew, in the Garden Room and there would be the overnight stay in order to be with him the next day as they became acquainted. What if he only reserved one room? On that her mind was made up. She would come home and never see him again.

Apprehensive, Suze began to pack the suitcase. What did one wear to a first meeting? She wanted to look attractive but not seductive. Seductive? Where did that come from? She wondered as she caught a glimpse of herself in the mirror across the room… and giggling, she struck a pose. "Girl, you just don't have it. You are a small town girl washed in the tradition of a thousand years. But there's always hope." Stepping out of her comfort zone, tomorrow she would meet him. Lord have mercy on her soul.

* * * * * * *

Outside the sprinklers were wanding magic on the lawn, a green oasis in an otherwise scorched world. Suze had arrived to find the room reserved, just as he said, spacious and cool in spite of the heat. She hung the garments, placed the suitcase inside the closet and closed the door. A bit antsy, she changed in to the light yellow dress, combed her hair into place and sparingly touched a drop of Illusion behind each ear, her wrists and there in the hollow of her neck. With her dark hair and brown eyes the yellow frock was becoming, its softness draping easily over her body. She was well aware, the weight loss since Wade's death made her appear wasp thin and her matronly facets had disappeared along with the pounds. None of that mattered; she had salvaged enough clothes from her collection to keep going.

"You look like a model," Mabel's words rang in her memory. Mabel found herself round and curvy while Suze was straight as a stick. Suze had to smile. Mabel was a good friend but she'd kept this little rendezvous to herself. Rendezvous, huh? On that, reaching for the wide brimmed hat, Suze slipped quietly out the door, ready to find a secret spot where she could sit and watch the people in the lobby and wait for him to arrive. Across the room there was one other person, a wide shouldered man sipping coffee and reading his newspaper. The three piece suit made her wonder what his business was in the Cape. Wearing suits was rare back in Newhaven, saved in the closet for holidays, namely Easter and Christmas.

The Gates House

"I'm leaving," Daniel found Ellen in the kitchen studying the calendar. "That's a lot of markings; do you know what they mean?" He leaned to kiss her. "Fraid I gotta go to work, Missus Gates," he teased. "How's that for the delivery boy. Does he kiss your cheek when he leaves?"

Ellen wrapped her arms around his neck. "What delivery boy? They're scared to death of these twins, now that the last two are walking, it's pandemonium around here." She grinned, her forehead to his, staring into his eyes. "Those markings are the helpfulness of Danny. Your namesake. Were you a busy boy when you were little?"

"Ah," taking the nearest chair, he pulled her onto his lap. "You will have to ask my aunt. I think I was a good boy." He tweaked her nose. "Were you a good little girl?"

She sighed, looking across the room to the hall that led to the boys room. "I hope but right now I pray those two sleeps late, I have so much to do."

"Like what?"

"Well, if Angeline comes early, I have to study my notes for the book review I'm doing for classes from our church in the Garden Room."

"The Garden Room and what book review?"

"Remember the book we read? The Harbinger?" He nodded. "Well, there's a work book that goes along with it and several classes have elected to do a comparison…" She was rising from his lap.

"Sounds involved." Standing, he reached for his brief case. "And you are chosen to help them devise a teaching plan." She shook her head negatively. "You are teaching a class in the Garden Room?"

"How did you know?" She smacked a good smoochy kiss on his lips. "Have a good day, Sir."

Daniel was holding his brief case arm's length from his body. "What is that on…."

Ellen was laughing. "I think… mashed potatoes from the twin's dinner last night. I thought I got it all."

"Those boys are going to bring us to our knees. How do they do all the things they do…and for that matter, how do you? We have our own team here and yet you are chosen." He paused. "Lotta work goes into book studies and all this busy-ness here." He paused, "it's the delivery boy helps, isn't it?"

She pushed him out the door as Ruthie climbed onto a stool at the island. "Do we have a delivery boy? I've never seen him." Ruthie studied the books she had brought from her room.

"Neither have I," Ellen grinned, pecking a kiss on Ruthie's forehead. "Thought you'd sleep late."

"Angeline's coming. I told her I'd help her read." A frown of concern lined her brow. "Do you think it's all right if Angeline learns to read from my books and not a reader? She loves The Secret Garden."

"I think it's wonderful you are teaching Angeline." Ellen paused for a moment. "The Secret Garden isn't just another fairy tale, it has meaning and yes, I think it is fine to help Angeline read from it. My Grandmother loved that book and probably read it at least once every year and she was quite elderly."

"Angeline's going to watch the twins while I do the book study, are you going with me?"

"Yes ma'm. I think I'm supposed to."

"Really?" Ellen stopped cleaning the legs of the table where she'd missed a spot from the night before.

"Do you know why?" Ellen understood completely what Ruthie was saying. She and Ruthie shared a gift, a gift from heaven, they often reminded each other, not to be used for gain but to bless or ease the path of others. "The gathering will be mostly regular church going attendees."

"I only know I'm to be there." Sliding off the stool, Ruthie headed back to her room. "I forgot something."

Within minutes, Angeline arrived for reading lessons in Ruthie's room, the older twins were hurrying down the hall and the peace and quiet of the early morning hours was broken. With one eye on the clock, Ellen realized if there were minutes to review notes for the book study, she had better make arrangements. The hour would arrive quicker than she anticipated.

Chapter Four

Suze studied the brick floor, the potted plants sitting by the tall rounded columns. The atmosphere reminded her of Louisiana on a good day, when the humidity wasn't striking one down. Glancing toward the front windows…her heart skipped a beat, beneath the portico a man was getting out of a brown Road Runner. Dressed casually, a white knit three button pullover made his tan obvious, the creased trousers, down to the tip of nicely polished shoes told the observer he had dressed with care.

Head down, Suze scooted her chair back behind the round column, wishing she had chosen a different place to sit. Casually she slipped the newspaper lying on the table, up, to cover her face as she listened to the conversation going on at the desk. "No," he was saying, "I'm not with the editor's convention." He gave a short laugh. "I'm here to meet a dear friend, before continuing my journey north." There the words became muffled as the girl behind the counter was listing information. She heard his name.

Relieved, when he returned to the vehicle, she lowered the newspaper and watched as he circled the portico and parked. Retrieving an overnight bag, he clicked the fob of keys in his hand and headed to the outer entrance. Suze felt the warmth wash over her and prayed she didn't break out in sweat, she was that nervous. What was she to do? Wait? Go to her room? A brief panic had built in the short time she observed him. What was she, a widow, doing here meeting a stranger?

He was nothing she had imagined, a short average man with an accent. No, he was taller than Wade; she guessed over six feet, his hair was beginning to silver just over the ears, otherwise dark and his skin was olive. He was handsome. Catching a glimpse of herself in the vein mirrored wall, she appeared pale, scared and plain. Was there a chance she could slip upstairs, retrieve her personal belongings and drive away? But he would track her down. She had already learned he was tenacious. Instead, she gripped her hands together, stared to one side saying a prayer; a prayer for help and possibly invisibility.

"Excuse me?" The accent, purred between them. "My Lady? Suze?"

She turned to meet his direct brown eyes, the mouth smiling and revealing perfect white teeth. He extended a hand. She placed her hand in his as she arose. His smile widened. "You're beautiful, I like what I see," he said. "Suze, I'm so happy to meet you, at last. My Lady." His voice was soft as velvet with a reverent touch on each word. He leaned to place a kiss on her cheek. "Excuse my choice of words," he apologized. "I'm afraid I built quite a case of nerves as I drove here, so anxious to meet you."

For the first time, Suze relaxed and a smile played upon her features. "You are very beautiful, Suze." His accent was warm and inviting; his tone sincere, his expression pleasing. Suze blushed. She didn't know what to say. He understood, reaching for her hand, he smiled. Glancing at the watch on his wrist, for a moment his eyes questioned the hour, "What can we do, my lady? I am unfamiliar with your town. Is there a river walk? We could stroll as we become acquainted?" He tilt his head, "Is that a good suggestion, or no?"

She nodded; thankful she had brought a hat for when the sun rose higher. "We can walk," she said, "It isn't far."

"I was told all American girls wear boy's breeches, now. But you wear a dress. Do you always?"

Her laughter was spontaneous. "I'm afraid we do like the freedom of wearing trousers, but I mix the two. My mother was old fashioned, she thought girls should prove they were ladies and wear dresses."

"Uh, huh," he said, his mind accepting this piece of information. "I like your mother's theory."

"You are from Spain?"

"Yes, originally, my birth," he replied. "But because of my work I have had residence in your country."

"Tell me about your mother." They were reaching the wall, painted in beautiful scenes by the University's promising artist. If one focused on the wall, their world was one of gardens, street scenes reminiscent of Italy, the dreams of a younger generation unfolding before their eyes, beautiful and often a sense of yearning captured by one's own feeling of delight. "Shall we rest a moment?" One of a dozen concrete table and benches was at their disposal. He nodded and waited for her to be seated.

"My mother," he said, his eyes looking into the past. "Was a very beautiful woman with black hair and eyes that danced as she told her stories of the family? Because she wanted me to know my family." He paused, "You understand? In Spain we are not all rich. My parents fell in love at a very young age. They had only each other and life was difficult to make ends meet. But they loved each other and they loved me."

"You said was. Does that mean your mother has…"

"Passed on," he said. "When I was twelve my Poppa was hurt, a job related accident and the company gave my mother money when he died. But she was too broken hearted to understand what to do with it. It was winter, my mother would walk in the rain and it was cold. She became sick with pneumonia and died." He sighed. "I was twelve. I was forced to work the streets. There was the money in the bank but I could not touch it until I was eighteen, and only then because she specifically noted such…and when I could, I used the nominal amount to receive an education and became an engineer." He sighed. "I much would have preferred to have my mother." His eyes held with hers, seeking understanding.

She was quiet.

"You have family? Children?"

"No."

"You were married?"

"Yes, my husband died."

"I am very sorry," he said gently, "My Lady." Rising, he again reached for her hand and did not release it as they walked. "May I see you again, tomorrow?" He stopped walking. "All these months I have wondered what you would say to me, what your appearance, whether you would like me and if you would not be scared because I talk different." His eyes bore into hers. "It is important to me you like me." Now he smiled to break the sternness of his words. "Do you know yet, if you like me?"

His smile was infectious. "I'm very cautious," she replied.

"I know. I know." His voice revealed an anxious need. "You tried too many times to turn me away. Why?"

"I live in a small community where everyone makes assumption of one's life. I don't want them second guessing me or what I'm doing."

"You are afraid?" Those dark eyes pierced her very soul. "Oh, my lady, that is not good. How can I break the barrier? You fear what people would say? It is none of their business. You are a lady." She did not reply. "I will move very slow, my Suze. But if it is possible, I believe I have fallen for you and the very essence of being with you is pleasing."

Suze pulled her hand from his. Anxiety was written all over her face. She wanted to cry. "I cannot …" Commit myself, she was thinking wildly, but he was studying her. "I have to go," she said. "Please."

"No, no, no." His arm went loosely around her, cupping her shoulder in a slight gesture. "We will speak no more of deep desire. I will court you, my Suze and in the end you will understand my delight in today; meeting you, dear lady and my willingness to take as long as it will take to win you. Now let us walk and you will tell me of your family, your dearly beloved husband who has passed and about your city. I want to know what makes you happy. Surely you have a hobby, a like of something special."

Suze rejected the idea of telling him about Wade and was reluctant to discuss anything even remotely dear to her. His warmth and complete interest was a winning factor, however, whether for her or not she wasn't certain but by noon they had walked the length of the painted wall, pausing to rest now and then to sit on the benches and as the sun rose in the sky and they started back a friendship of sorts began. Once, her love of gardening slipped into the conversation. She prayed the slip went unnoticed.

"This time tomorrow," he said, as they lingered in the Cape's Garden Room, over lunch. "Sadly I will be leaving you. If I'm to make my company's yearly meeting, I must." His words dropped softly as he reached for her hand and gave it a slight squeeze. "I hope you will miss me, my lady. I know I shall certainly miss you." Across the room a group of ladies clapping drew Suze attention. Withdrawing her hand, she was at a loss for words; not only with his sincerity but that one of the ladies was coming to their table. There was a faint recognition to someone she knew she had met. And here she was…with him and he completely unaware of her discomfort as he continued speaking.

"Could you come to my city, the last of November as I will have returned by Thanksgiving?" He leaned forward to secure her attention. "If you will, all arrangements will be complete for your stay and I shall return your visit by coming to the Cape for the Christmas holidays," he hesitated, "if it meets your approval." He felt she was completely unsettled to the idea. "You feel I move too…" He searched for a word. "Too soon? Too fast?" Something was beginning to click in his mind that her focus was on the lady now standing next to her and Suze would like nothing better than to run away or sink into the floor. She appeared nervous. Finally, he realized meeting him had brought her completely out of her comfort zone. While the lady was speaking, Suze had gone pale and unresponsive.

"Hello, Mrs. Norman. Do you remember me?"

"Ellen Gates," Suze stammered, her eyes sweeping from Ellen to….she had no idea at this moment his name. "My friend," she said, her eyes locked on his face as he arose courteously extending his hand.

"Stephen Silvi," he said."Do you care to join us?"

"No, thank you," Ellen replied. "I'm here to help with a book study and saw Mrs. Norman and just wanted to say hello. If you wish to join us, we would make you welcome." Her smile turned into laughter."How are you spending your afternoon?"

"I'm afraid I don't know your city," Stephen replied, "And Suze is reluctant to make suggestion. I thought perhaps if there, how I shall say this, perhaps a park, or a place of beautiful landscaping. In my country we have gardens we explore to walk and become acquainted. I think Suze enjoys…"

"Of course," Ellen's smile widened. "When we were in Newhaven, someone pointed out a beautifully kept yard and it was

Mrs. Norman's. I haven't forgotten." She thought for a moment. "I really don't think there's any place here in the Cape." Her smile widened. "Unless you would like to tour the garden my husband is building for me…and we do have a friend with the most beautiful rose garden."

"That is too private, Ms. Gates. Ellen," Suze stuttered. "We could not impose." She was shaking her head. "You hardly know us."

"We have the same heavenly Father," Ellen said softly. She took a small card from her pocket. "Here's my address and I'll give Harriet a call just in case you decide you would like to see her rose garden. It's on the oldest street in town, old bricks, sprawling oak trees and stately mansions. I used to live in one" She grinned. "But mine was in much need of repair and a few years later a friend refurbished it."

Stephen was warming to the idea. He handed Ellen a pen and she scribbled her friends address on back. "I promise you won't be bored. There's an unforgettable angel in our backyard garden. Do go see it." She was turning toward the group she had left, "Nice to meet you and I'll give Harriet a call right now." With a twinkle of her fingers, Ellen produced a cell and was dialing as she walked away.

Stephen had to laugh; Suze was biting her lip while a rosy glow had come into her cheeks. "I must admit, I much better like you blushing than turning pale and I'm happy to meet your friend. Ellen?"

Clasping her hands together, Suze replied, "I barely know her. Twice we've been in church together."

"Then you know her and obviously she wishes for you to see her garden." There was a twinkle in his eye. "Come. Let us go."

Chapter Five

A reluctant Suze followed him to the brown Road Runner. Inside was immaculate and she was beginning to form a picture of him as a very neat man, by the way he handled the napkin at the table, little things you barely notice, she thought, but still you do. She being an organized person didn't mind; but in her own world, sometimes she left a thing undone for a more pressing matter learning that after Wade's death. A sigh pressed its way from her lips as she glanced at the roadside. Life without Wade was hard. From keeping the car filled with gas, to having someone come to repair the things that seemed to be falling apart without him, life had its moments and she was finding it wasn't the big things that broke her spirit, big things had to be fixed; it was the endless little things that brought anxiety and tears.

"You are in distress, my lady?" There was a compassionate tone in his voice and his eyes.

"When your wife died, what did you miss most," She asked.

"Her." He replied without pause. "Knowing the person who loved me, listened to me, my person was gone." He glanced her way. "And you?"

"The same." Again, she sighed, "Just knowing he would come home nights. That was a comfort."

"Yes." He had entered Ellen's address into the system, but was surprised when they turned into a more secluded neighborhood with larger lots and privacy to each home. "Very nice," he said, pulling to the side of the street. "In case the owner arrives to shew us out of his garden," he laughed. "Now I'm feeling a bit uncertain…but your Ellen did invite us to her garden, did she not?" He removed the keys, climbed from the vehicle and was quickly opening Suze door. "Ah, the garden gate," he pointed ahead.

"Oh." Suze first impression was one of awe. "I've never seen this in anyone's landscape. It is absolutely breath taking." She was drawn to the sound of water. Behind a stone wall a cherub on a huge carved bowl was sending out water that traveled a circle returning to be recycled again and again. Banks of perennials brought color and life to the setting with a stone bench to one side and an engraved plaque that bore the words, "The water I give them will become in them a spring of water welling up to eternal life." John 4:14

"Do you understand the meaning of the writing?" He was dipping his fingers in the water. "There's another over here." He led her to the spot where the water turned and read aloud, "Whoever believes in me, Out of his heart will flow rivers of living water." She was silent. He was waiting.

"Do you know Jesus?"

He stared at her thinking, she could not read his expression, how was he to answer profound question?

"What do you mean?"

She touched her heart. "In here, do you know him? Has he claimed your life and you live his example?"

"What you mean his example?" The studied art of language slipped away as he listened intently.

"Let us sit here on the bench," she said, wondering at her own intention to explain and even more wondering where the boldness to feel she could explain was coming from. "These words are from Bible scripture."

"I know Bible." He nodded.

"Do you believe in Jesus Christ? Have you given your heart to him, to follow the example he set for us?" They were so intent speaking they did not see the child coming their way from the house.

"Is that necessary? My country is Catholic, we believe, that is all. I believe. I cannot speak for others." He questioned the meaning. "Believing is different, it is important?"

"It is what you believe, it is not denominational. Believing Christ died for our sins and rose again, that is very important…but giving him our heart is more." Her eyes filled with caring. "When I was a child I realized I loved the Lord. I believed the scripture but I didn't know how to act on what I was feeling. Then there was a revival and an altar call that I answered."

"How did you answer?" He was leaning forward, listening intently. "This I've not before heard."

"If I had a Bible I could show you scripture." It was then they heard the laughter of a child and turned to see a young girl approaching. "Hello," Suze called to her. "We met your mother, we have permission…"

"Yes, yes." Ruthie extended her hand to Suze. "My mother called to say you would arrive. I'm Ruthie. I decided not to go with my mother today. We met when my parent's led music at your church revival." Ruthie grinned. "I kept the twins out of trouble." Now she waited for Suze to introduce her friend, but when she did not, Ruthie extended her hand to him, also. "Do you like my parent's garden?"

"It is most beautiful," he bowed over her hand. "My name is Stephen."

"I heard you say you wished for a Bible," Ruthie motioned for them to follow her and led them down the path to the large angel that centered the whole garden, and raised the seat at its feet. "My mother comes here daily to pray and she wants a bible kept here." She turned to leave but Suze spoke.

"Would you help me explain to my friend why we give our heart to Jesus and that is only part of believing?" Suze wanted him to understand and she knew from the Bible study, Ruthie could do it.

Ruthie reached to take Stephen's hand. "It is our path to salvation," she said. "Believing in Christ Jesus and asking his forgiveness for our sins is the first step; second is believing that he died on the cross for our sins and third that Jesus Christ rose from death. It is believing but then it is following the commandments he laid out for us to live by. Do you understand?"

Stephen was lost in the soft voice of the child but there was a feeling of rest coursing through his body as she held his hand, a feeling he could not understand. He thought he had masked his feelings from Suze very well but it was as though this child shredded those things he remembered. He was stripped bare to the soul by a child… it was more than he could comprehend and now he stumbled at her question. He had not been completely truthful with Suze but then he did not know if she would accept truth now. This child represented innocence and complete trust in what she was explaining to him.

"Do you understand, Stephen?" It was Suze's voice calling him back from the wanderings of his mind. He shook his head, as one would come up from water's depth. She was studying him in a curious way.

"Yes. Yes, my lady," he said, his accent thick as it was mornings when he first awakened.

"You understand about salvation, Stephen?" Her voice sounded worried. The child let go of his hand, smiling as she was ready to leave. Feeling a strange quiet within, Stephen wondered if he was the same.

"You seem," Suze tilt her head, "I don't know…how you seem… are you all right?"

"This garden, the angel reminds me of my thoughts of you when we say goodbye." Something made him reluctant to share, for fear of rejection. "When I say to you, I send love on angel's wings." He glanced quickly to Suze. "The example of that love, more pure is in this garden. How does one have the insight to build a garden like this? I desire to know the meaning of the writings on the stone."

"All I've ever heard about the Gates is that they are good people and their little daughter…" Suze paused. "She came with her mother when Mrs. Gates led in Bible study; it was our best study ever."

"If you don't mind, let us go back to the hotel and perhaps plan something special tonight." He peered at her to see if that met her approval. "And tomorrow morning, I shall be gone by the time you awaken. We will say our goodbyes tonight." His very serious eyes did not leave her. "Does that meet your approval, my lady?" He needed a moment to consider what he was feeling in his spirit.

Suze nodded, though her mind was busy considering his change in the last hour's happenings. There was something different and she couldn't put her finger on exactly when the change occurred; perhaps when the little girl came and touched him; she remembered the women at the Bible Study saying the little girl seemed to radiate goodness and yes, peace and calm and there was a very secret rumor that said the child was a gifted one, whether she sensed situations or the Lord truly gave her insight, no one really knew. It was further mentioned the child's friends and family protected her from would be soothsayers that would try to gain fame by association with one who was gifted by God.

"The writing on the stones are scripture." It was coming to her mind, possibly he was experiencing things he was at a loss to understand and she could not explain. "I could have returned home." She said.

"No, my lady, we must have the night. What harm is there that we have more time together?"

Suze would return to the night's events many times in the future and always there would be a puzzling consideration; he was charming but Stephen Silvi was withholding something from her that she should know. He had spoken of truth and trust on their way back to the hotel and understanding scripture.

The Gates Home

"Ruthie, did the people come to visit our garden?"

"Yes, Momma, they did."

"What did you think about them?" Ellen paused to hear her daughter's reply.

"They were surprised to see me." Ruthie glanced up from sitting the table. "I know you invite people to our garden because it's calm and peaceful and daddy worked hard on it but what if they don't like it??"

Ellen chuckled. "I never thought of that before. Did Mrs. Suze and her friend not like our garden?"

"She loved it. I felt his spirit struggling. He said a lot of work was in it, so I don't know."

"He got that right." Ellen sit a bowl of mashed potatoes on the table. "If you will call your brothers, Dad should be home any time now." A thought occurred. "Maybe her friend isn't a Christian."

"He's troubled. I felt it and Mrs. Suze wonders what's wrong but she won't ask."

"How old are you?" Ellen sit the green beans on the table and reached to pull Ruthie into her arms.

* * * * *

Newhaven

Nate was becoming a regular visiting Mabel weekdays when they would sit out on the front porch in those grand old rockers listening to band students practicing songs for Harvest Rendezvous. Other schools brought their bands in to combine on the fields marching and playing their instruments as they made different formations that left the football crowd hollering for more. But today was practice and sometimes they marched down the street in front of Mabel's house.

"Britany has been offered a job." Turning to Mabel, Nate asked, "Did she tell you?"

"No. I'm surprised she didn't." Mabel sighed. "It hasn't been easy getting her to open up. She's not that difficult as a house guest but whatever drug Walden had her and Herm on must have altered their capabilities, sometimes I notice her staring into space. I ask, are you all right? She gives me this look and leaves the room. Maybe it will help if she has something to go to every day."

Nate scratched his head, a woeful expression on his face. "According to the grapevine she turned it down." It was obvious he was disappointed. "Said she had other plans. What's going to happen to her? First she wants another woman's husband, and then she ties in with Walden and Smith to retaliate Matt's rejection." He gripped the arms of the chair as if to rid himself of some terrible fear. "Here she is, a girl with potential; graduated with high honors, got her degree started teaching at the academy, all right, but got involved with a male teacher, there, and they asked her to leave that school."

"I don't know what to say, Nate. I've been as good to her as if she was my own, but she holds back."

"So you have no idea where she goes each month?"

"Not a clue. She just slips away."

For a spell they sit in silence, their chairs rocking in unison, noticing the flow of traffic and one car in particular, their heads turning as Suze passed by, waving and going on to her own drive.

"Wonder where she's been," Mabel said. "I called this morning and got her answering machine. I know she has an appointment with her dentist this month at the Cape."

"Suze is an innocent," Nate replied. "Too sweet to do anything clandestine."

"Suze is a good Christian woman who loved her husband dearly."

"You are saying Suze would never consider another man?"

"Loneliness is a strange bed fellow, Nate."

"What about you, Mabel? Would you consider another man?"

"Well," Mabel laughed, a spontaneous sound that made Nate smile. "I considered you, didn't I?"

"A younger man would ask you if you were ready to take the next step," Nate cleared his throat. "I'm older now, Mabel, but I do wonder from time to time, if an older man…in time… ask an older woman to marry, what do you suppose she'd say?"

Mabel's face was flushed as a nervous laugh issued from within her as if on its own. "Why, Nate…We are both in good health now, but what happens when we aren't?"

"That's a strange reply, Mabel. We take care of each other." He rose from the chair. "Think about it, Mabel. Time is passing. Haven't we wasted a good amount of our life?"

"Wasn't yours a happy marriage? If so, nothing was wasted."

"What does that have to do with anything?" His expression was troubled.

"I didn't, Nate. A woman considers everything. You deserve the best."

"I've always known the best was you." He slipped his hand into his pocket to find his keys. "Take your time. We will begin a formal courtship and when you feel enough time has passed, let me know."

Chapter Six

Britany drove past the home, his home, the place where he lived with his wife who was expecting a second child, another addition to Matt's family. Did he want the new baby? Was he happy? His mother said no, he wasn't happy. What about the little boy, she asked Vivien, whose reply had been, I hardly know him. Assuming he is Matt's son, but it doesn't matter. When you marry Matt, then I'll have grandchildren.

Parking in the shade of one of the huge oak trees, Britany studied the century old house. Matt's home where he lives with her when he isn't working the farm for his father, she thought. Could that be the indication that he really wasn't a happy man? What husband and father left his family? Matt was there last harvest and would be for this one. Start to finish he had over-seen the crop progress from planting to harvest which was now ready to begin.

Vivien Langley was her friend but in her present circumstance, Britany, truthfully, did not understand a grandmother who dismissed her grandchildren so easily. Shouldn't she want to see them, embrace them because they were a part of not only her son but of her and Bill. Their blood line ran through the children's veins, didn't it?

Hands clenching the steering wheel, Britany lay her head against it. Thinking was an ordeal since Walden had given her the mind altering drug. How she ever fell in with his lot she would never understand. At her lowest point in life, she supposed she had been vulnerable.

The pity party swept through her mind and coursed her body to claim her heart and soul, and once more she felt completely alone and adrift in the world. Since losing both parents, she found no meaning to anything. She tried to function as she believed they would want, but there was no joy. Matt said she had built more into their relationship than friendship and she had. The Academy kicked her out because she and one of their teachers became involved, that was the first step to her downfall, then Matt's rejection followed by Walden's seduction.

All the while to the world she had functioned as a responsible person, attending church, even buying a new piano for the Sanctuary, which they would not let her play. It all built into a mass of warring emotions that had nearly destroyed her. The stay in the hospital had brought back reality but she had a long way to go and now this....

Sheltered from prying eyes she watched the neighborhood come alive. School buses crossed the intersection, doors opened, children hopped down the steps and headed for their home on the street. And then it was five o'clock and still she sat there. Suburban's with male drivers for the most part, gave a hasty stop at the sign and hurried on. For the first time she chuckled, saying aloud, "the bread earner is headed home." A wicked laugh followed, "Daddy's home." She met her eyes in the mirror and smirked at their diabolical gleam. "Naughty, naughty." She wagged a finger in the air. "Naughty."

A deep sigh enveloped her body. Of course she should head home. For a brief spell she was ward of the court, at her age, ward of the court and could not stay alone which was a big laugh because they were now letting her drive to her doctor's appointment in the Cape. By night, she was supposed to be back at Mrs. Mable Hisaw's home, the lady appointed to be her guardian, until she could stand on her own. Humiliation was no respecter of persons. Her parents would have been mortifiably embarrassed.

She had no idea how long she sat there. Keying the engine, she knew she must move on; the hand inside the glassed dashboard did not move, no sound emitted from the engine, nothing happened. Opening the door, she stepped out of the vehicle, rounded to the front and tried to raise the hood. A shiny black suburban pulled behind her car, two men simultaneously climbed out coming to help her. The blonde guy in the tan suit raised the hood, the second more casually dressed, his hair pulled back in a ponytail reached down into the depth of motor and pulled out an oil stick. "It's good," he said.

"Have this problem often," Pony tail guy asked. Glancing at the battery cables, he said, "They're good."

Both men were waiting for her answer. "I think the battery is dead," she said.

They gave each other meaningful glances as the pony tail guy went to the back of the Suburban to return with a set of cables. The blonde male pulled the Suburban alongside. It was a matter of attaching the cable to posts and in a short few minutes the engine hummed.

"Better get the vehicle out of the traffic lane," the one said, saluting as the other stowed the cables and was getting into the passenger side when Britany caught up with them.

"Thank you."

The two smiled as the pony tail guy handed her a card, while his friends was pulling away. Sliding under the wheel, she hastily read the names printed in raised black lettering. Andrew Graves Attorney at Law. Pookie Fernandez Lawyer in training. She had to chuckle. No self-respecting lawyer would print that on his business card. She read the second line; Business with a purpose, confidentiality our calling card. Laughing, she stuck the card in the side pocket of her purse. Who knew, she might need a lawyer one day. "I'll write the Pony tail guy a thank you note." He had that strange macho appeal she liked.

She drove past city limits, headed toward Newhaven and Mabel Hisaw's home. Her time there was almost finished and then she was on her own. A terrible loneliness streaked through her mind. It imprisoned her; she felt incapable to do anything with her life and she wondered that others did not see the sadness she felt. Alone. Alone. Alone. She pounded the steering wheel, and made the car cross the line, corrected and swerved in so doing. Just her luck, a white car went into motion, lights flashing, as it pulled in behind her. She hadn't seen the Patrol car, how stupid could she get? She pulled over.

An hour later Mrs. Hisaw asked, "Have you had a good day, Britany?" She shrugged her shoulders and went to her room. Dead battery stopped by the highway patrol and bad news. Her day was normal.

The Cape

It was pure pandemonium. Ruthie was near tears. Ellen came inside from the garden. "What Is going on?" The twins had poured every toy from the toy basket and were now struggling with each other over an old stuffed rabbit dressed in overalls and wearing a hat. But the ears that held the hat on the rabbits head were sorely tattered at this point barely hanging by a thread. One more pull and she feared there would be no way to keep the hat or ears and wondered they were still there, anyway. She walked to the center of the room, pulled one child into each arm and ask, "What is this all about?"

"It's my rabbit. He lost his. It's gone. He flushed it down the toilet." Fresh tears sprang from Danny's eyes. "Make him leave me alone, Momma. I don't like him."

"Then, you must not like me because I like him, of course I like you, too. I love you both." She held onto them. Danny tried to get loose but succumbed finally to lay his head on her shoulder and sob. This made Sammy cry. "Why are you crying?" Leaning her head she stared into Sammy's face. "Answer me. Why are you crying?"

"I want my rabbit. I didn't throw it in the commode. It fell in… but…"

"Who flushed the commode and stopped up everything until Daddy came home from work that night?"

"We did," the boys said in unison, appearing to be very proud they accomplished the act. "We did it."

Closing her eyes, Ellen tried not to laugh. Dan had pulled a very water logged and somewhat worse for the wear Mr. Whiskers from the commode, shaking his head and wondering what was next. "I have good news and bad," she said. "Now look at me. No struggles, just look at me while I speak to you."

"But I want my rabbit." Tears continued to streak down Sammy's face.

"Shh," Ellen cautioned. "I have to punish you for fighting because you don't listen. I want you to go back to your room, remove your shoes and lie down on your bed. I'll set the timer and you may get up when it goes off. Fair enough, huh? Maybe you won't fight again."

"What's the good news?" Danny clutched his bunny tighter to his chest, waiting.

Ellen stared down at her boys. "The good news is this, Daddy retrieved Sammy's Mr. Whiskers but after going through the washing machine he is a bit different…and of course his stay in the commode didn't help." She rose up, sighing. "If you are in your beds, I'll get Mr. Whiskers, but if you aren't, no one gets their bunny."

She was back in the kitchen, for the moment no sound was coming from the boy's bedroom, both were in bed clutching their rabbits. Pouring a cup of coffee, Ellen settled down at the table and reached for her bible for the morning's devotion, when the phone rang.

"Yes, this is she." She listened, as a frown creased her brows. "Well, yes, I do know Mrs. Norman. But can't you send the hat to her?" She was informed they had no address because the gentleman made the reservation and paid for both rooms and they were asked not to bother the lady for details. "In that case, then", Ellen said, "Yes, I will be responsible for seeing Mrs. Norman's hat is returned to her. But let me give you her number and you can call her and see what she wants done. You are welcome." She hung up the phone and stared down into the brown liquid in her cup. "Another task."

Ruthie shuffled into the room; her rabbit faced house shoes made Ellen smile. "I see you have your bunnies, too."

Grinning, Ruthie slid into the chair opposite her. "Are you going to see Mrs. Norman, Momma? May I go with you to see Mrs. Merkal?" Ruthie was pouring cereal into a bowl. "I really like Mrs. Merkal."

"To tell you the truth, I want to check first with Marigold and if she has a trip down to Newhaven, then I will ask her to deliver the hat, if not we will go. How's that?" Ellen sighed, "But Daddy will have to keep the boys."

Newhaven's Shining Light Church

"There you are." Mabel stepped to where Suze was busy counting out pieces of donated material large enough to make lap pads. "You are pretty involved, there, need some help?"

"I'm trying to pair small cuts together in pairs and we need sixteen sets. Some of these pieces are not large enough for a dwarf but I guess there are toddlers in hospitals from time to time could use those large bibs. What do you think?"

"Sounds good to me." Mabel hesitated and then asked, "Suze have I offended you in any way, because if I have I'm ready to apologize. We've not seen each other for over a week now and I've missed you."

"My heavens, no. No." Suze emphasized the word, turning to study Mabel. She couldn't very well say "my mind's distracted by a man who ends his text;"I send my love on angel wings" could she?

"I called, Suze, but when you didn't answer I wondered if you went to the Cape for your dentist appointment. How are your teeth, anyway?"

They both laughed. Suze wanted to discuss her evening at the Garden Room but Mabel might tease or worse lecture her on the danger of meeting a man she met on the internet, so she kept quiet. Mabel considered for a moment telling Suze about Nate's last words, a formal courtship had begun between the two, but Suze might feel their friendship threatened because Mabel would be spending more time with Nate and she already had the feeling Suze felt more alone than ever, so she kept quiet.

They were half way through the sewing meeting when Miss Talulah came to the door and motioned for Suze to join her. "There's a call from you in the office. A man." Talulah remained calm, though her mind was in a whir. Suze avoided the men of the congregation. It was more than she could comprehend, Suze having a relationship with a new man? When Suze laughed she knew that was her signal to return.

"That's so strange," Suze explained. "When I was last at the Cape, I left my hat. Long story short, someone found it and they want to return it. I shall be pleasantly surprised." Talulah heard the tingle in Suze voice as it lilt above the others. "They said a person in the Cape was coming to Newhaven and might bring it to me."

Yes, definitely a man, Talulah was thinking. After all the lonely years of her own life she was an expert on the matter. There would be clandestine meetings where nothing happened, a handshake, a how are you today inquirement and then nothing but empty days stretching into years. Talulah straightened the jacket over her pencil skirt, tucked a stray hair back into the bun at the nape of her neck and gave the Pastor a sultry eyed don't you bother me, buster, look as she passed him in the hall. What did they think women had ice water running through their veins?

Men now days chose younger women and older ones went through life looking as if they enjoyed seeing the mess they made. Her lips curled in a delicious smile, while laughter bubbled up in her chest. Let them marry their younger women…and raise them. Laughter echoed down the hall to where Pastor Levi turned to see his secretary disappearing into the office.

He was scared of her. Talulah Cohen found strength in her power over the ministers that passed through Shining Light Church. They didn't call her Tully for nothing. She knew the sins of every member. Once she had a secret love, but he turned into a regular scalamonger. You had to separate the goats from the lambs and he was a goat. She doubted to this day whether he was saved. She might be saucy but she believed in the Lord. You had to, to deal with the young pastors, the wayward girls and the redundant old men in a congregation.

Her laughter filled the office; she must put those sacrilegious thoughts out of mind. Shining Light was void of redundant old men, but a few wayward girls passed through, for instance that Britany girl. Thank goodness she didn't take interest in Jake Hutchens; now he and Laurie were ready to welcome a new baby into their home. Come spring Pastor Levi and Leah would do the same; God's mercy in view. She guessed two new babies was enough because the Barnes already had theirs.

Sliding into her chair behind the Victorian desk she had wanted so badly, Tully reached for the calendar. Tomorrow, the young woman who had cleared the debris after the church burnout and produced a beautiful sanctuary from the ashes would be stopping by. For a moment her mind lingered on that one. Ready to pop. It must be time for her to deliver, but she wasn't part of Shining Light, that young lady attended Christ Church at the Cape. Tully couldn't fault the girl. The sanctuary was peaceful and calming, if she'd decorated it, it might have turned into a fiasco.

She was Matt Langley's wife. Poor thing that meant Vivien was her mother in law. Poor thing.

Chapter Seven

At her Cape Shoppe Marigold walked the room slowly perusing the cases. Opting for tables, the glassed cases held more expensive items among them the new silver line of bracelets and chains. Again, Harriet insisted she carry the line before another shop claimed it. It was turning into the calling card of the shop after she ran the add and a coupon stating twenty five percent off.

It surprised her high school girls were buying the line, with the lowest price no less than twenty five dollars. "They work," Harriet stated, "and they want the real thing, no substitute. Just be happy they've found you. It's a different world, Marigold, now we pander to the teenagers. That's what style is all about, being young…anyway looking young."

"But a pair of simple earrings cost twenty five dollars?"

"They are silver, Marigold. Sterling silver."

"They might turn," she muttered. "Everything turns."

"Just tell me what's on your mind. It's time for the baby, so I know you are speaking in regard to her arrival, aren't you? You don't mean Matt, do you? Because he promised he would be here." Harriet leaned into the pile of letter jackets she was folding. "Are you worried about the delivery?"

"No." Marigold walked to the back. Harriet followed. "As time draws near, I think about the last time and how Matt wished his folks would show up, put the problem behind them and be a second set of grandparents to M.J." She sighed. "But it didn't happen and it won't. Again."

"Why are you dwelling on this?"

"Because I love my husband. He's a good man and he deserves their respect in regards to M.J. and me." Tears welled up in her eyes. "Is there anything justified in his willingness to give up being apart from us to work for them?" Marigold slumped down into the old office chair she inherited with the shop. "It's not fair."

"I agree but I don't know the answer. Maybe the only answer is don't give up praying."

Blowing out built up steam, Marigold pushed the chair around and pulled it closer to the desk, to lay her head on a stack of bills. "I'm so tired, today, Ma. What do you think is wrong with me?"

"I don't know but maybe you should cancel that trip to Newhaven or let someone else take the supplies."

"I can't. I'm the one made the deal to restore everything and I'm on the last item to mark off the list."

"How about I go with you?"

"You have to stay here and run the shop." When the phone rang Harriet gave Marigold a hurried glance and went to answer it. Smiling when she returned, she waited for Marigold to ask why. "What?"

"Ellen and Ruthie are taking a ride down to the very little town we've been discussing and she would be happy to drop by the church if there's a need, because Ruthie wants to ride along to see the Pastor's wife." Harriet reached to pull Marigold out of the chair. "Come on, over here you can rest better."

"They've become close, almost as close as me and Ruthie…but we have history. I wish Ruthie would come by and lay hands on me, I hate to admit it, but I'm that unsettled inside and Ruthie's touch…"

"Do I need to call Matt?" worry lines claimed Harriet's brow. "Someone else could take his place."

"Not likely, Ma." Marigold tried to settle on one side of the last wicker chaise marked down for summer clearance. "They don't put inexperienced drivers on that expensive equipment."

Harriet threw her hands in the air. "I don't know how to help you."

"Just let me sit here, lay here, however I can get comfortable. Oh, Ma, this is good."

"You think you're getting by with this Ma stuff, but I'm aware of it." Harriet turned toward the packing table. "I plan to pack up the items you have on the table, assuming those are the items going to Shining Light, right? And then, I'm going to take them to Ellen. She said she would deliver and we are going to let her." She glanced across the room, then shook her head. Marigold was asleep.

The fatigue was becoming serious. A call to her doctor was in order and Harriet was the one to do it. When the phone rang again, Harriet caught it on the second ring.

"Hello, Gorgeous, this is the day I get to put my arms around you and as the song says, kiss your ruby red lips."

Harriet stifled a giggle, letting the silence grow.

"Marigold?" Alarm sounded in Matt's voice. "Babe, are you all right?"

"It's me, Matt. Harriet."

"Sorry about that, Ma. I was so anxious to hear from her. Where is she? She's supposed to come see me…"

"I don't think so, Matt, not this afternoon." Harriet kept her eyes on Marigold as she took a deep breath. "She's really swollen, Matt. Maybe as much as when she entered the hospital to have M.J."

"Oh, no," Matt's heart skipped a beat as he brought the machine to a stop. "What do we need to do?"

"Can you come home? Marigold said she thought not, but I'm asking anyway, Matt. She seems to be sleepy like she was with M.J. and if you recall the doctor said that wasn't normal."

"She wanted to carry this baby full term. What do you think?"

"Come home, Matt, and we'll discuss it while Marigold is in with her doctor."

Matt didn't mince words with his crew. "I have to check on my wife. Last time when we had our son, we almost lost Marigold. Now, you know what you have to do. Keep your mind on the task at hand, no messin' up. I'll be back Monday if all goes well."

Checking in with Nate was easy. "I'll see you Monday, if all goes well," he said. "Keep her in your prayers. She's unique and I want to keep her and another thing, pray her doctor will see her with tomorrow being Saturday."

Nate grinned. "That she is," he agreed, "and you're pretty special too, and I will pray.

It was nine thirty when Matt pulled into the drive. A light was on in the kitchen. He entered quietly, hurried down the hall to find M.J. sound asleep next to his mother. In the moonlight, Matt studied his wife's features. One foot sticking out of the covers was swollen with a silvery sheen. Tomorrow, they'd see the doctor. Stepping out of his denims, Matt first carried M.J. into the next bedroom, lay him down and returned to slide into bed beside Marigold.

"Am I dreaming," she whispered. "No not tonight," Matt replied, taking her into his arms." We're going to the doctor in the morning." Snuggling closer, Marigold sighed and whispered, "Okay."

Pookie

Pookie held the thank you card at arm's length. "It's pretty. It smells good but what does it say?"

Andrew laughed. "Probably that you need glasses. Man! You're not even forty yet."

"It's this hard work, setting up this office, manual labor."

"That may affect your muscles but I doubt your eye sight." Andrew reached for the card, "Thank you for the boost and helping me the other day." He paused, finally to say her name. "Britany James."

"You know her?"

"I know about her." Andrew slid his feet full length in front of his body, tiredness was seeping into his bones, too. They had the weekend to have the office ready for full use on Monday when one of the biggest clients to their area would be in for consultation. Glancing around, Andrew nodded approving, "We are making head-way, can't have Winters and Oldham thinking we're some fly by night seat of your pants firm. What we accomplish with them sets the mark. You do have to wonder why they chose us, when there's at least five other prominent law firms in this town."

"You don't know them?" Pookie scratched his chin where three days growth of beard was beginning to itch. "I don't think I'm continuing this beard thing. Tonight, it's gone." He rolled his chair in front of Andrew. "Winters had a kid over-dosed last year. Oldham has a twenty year old I've heard is a buyer. I don't doubt it, he's got all kind of open sores on his arms and his face never clears up. So I'd say he's a user."

"What would that have to do with needing an attorney?" Andrew studied the picture of the president they'd hung on the wall. "You know, Donald is tilting to the left and that's a sign to us." He grinned as Pookie rose up, walked to the wall and straightened the picture. "We'll need a picture of a good Democrat to match Donald. You got any suggestions?"

"I'm thinking take Donald down and slap a picture of Beyonce' up there and maybe Elvis."

"Elvis is dead. And we will be too, if we don't get this mess cleaned up and do a little homework."

"I'm thinking I should make a phone call. This chic, had curb appeal. I think I need to get to know her."

"Britany James?" Andrew studied Pookie for a minute. "Just to let you know the last three guys she was entangled with got the wrong end of the stick. Be careful. She's dangerous."

"I didn't think you knew her." Pookie slid the chair under the desk, wiped the top of the desk off with the hem of his t-shirt and straightened the monitor to the computer. "I'll remember your caution, but me thinks the lady is a fox and I want to get to know her. It won't put you out, will it?"

Andrew shrugged. "Won't bother me, but the women in my friend group, they may think differently."

"I won't even bother to ask." Pookie found a bottle of glass cleaner. "I need a good clean cloth."

Matt and Marigold

Matt held her hand,"Be careful your foot doesn't slip off the runner. I wasn't thinking, bringing you in the truck. Those things are tricky."

"It's okay, Matt. I'm just glad you are here and that Dr. Mark made time to see me on his rounds."

"Does that mean you are going to do as the doctor says, more rest, less work, no wedges and maybe you won't have to deal with the fluid, because if it continues you will be in the hospital on bed rest."

"I got it." Marigold leaned her head against the back of the seat. "Could you just let me be happy that for once someone else is driving? I get so tired of having to take care of myself. Get gas. Be on time for work, take M.J. to school and if something goes wrong, I'm the one has to deal with it." Staring at Matt, as he rounded the truck and slid under the steering wheel, she said, "It's so good to have you home Farm Boy." Giving a satisfied sigh, she settled into the seat as he reached for her hand. "You have the prescriptions?" She relaxed when he nodded and patted his shirt pocket.

"Next stop, fill prescriptions." Matt leaned across to lightly kiss her lips. "I miss you Tinkerbell. Please don't get sick like before. This year I couldn't handle it. Do you know what I mean?"

"You mean your plate is full. It's that one more thing syndrome. The same way I feel about Britany James being around. Maybe my constitution is low, but being pregnant and M.J. still depending on me, I can't handle the stress that woman brings. Please don't tell me I have to be lovey-dovey when I'm not feeling it. I know that sounds unchristian…it's actually just very pregnant mom talking. I'm sorry."

"Well, last I heard from Nate, Britany is asserting herself. You know she had to stay with someone awhile after release from the hospital…and Miss Mable Hisaw took her in, but she's beginning to drive again and doesn't tell anyone where she's going."

"Any place away from us, right?" She saw the flicker of concern in Matt. "You still worry over her, don't you?"

"I assure you, it is nothing but having grown up with her, all those years, just a friendship and now we are in this mess. I can't believe loneliness could so warp a person, tho some think she's just selfish."

"I will be more comfortable if we don't have to deal with her, Matt."

"Maybe we won't, Babe."

"Let's just enjoy the weekend," she said, looking out the window, the homes flashing by and she wondered about Matt and M.J. and was she going to be able to carry this baby to term. Instead of voicing her worries she said, "It will be so good to have you by my side at church on Sunday. I think some of the people question if I have a husband."

"They know I was with you before."

"People forget, Matt. Have you heard the things they say about May and her girls?"

Matt laughed. "May has had a rough life, Marigold. Everyone knows her, from here to Newhaven and beyond. She has worked many places. But if you are referring to May's daughters each having their own father. That's probably true."

"I try not to judge. My parents were hippies."

"There are worse things to worry about than being a hippie, Babe. Once Nate and I were talking and he mentioned the Old Testament being full of men with God given talents that went wrong. Saul, King David, and Solomon, supposed to have all the wisdom in the world, look what happened to him."

Marigold began to laugh. "You think you have problems with one wife, how about three hundred?"

* * * * * * *

"Hey, Buddy," Matt woke to M.J. bouncing on the bed. He could hear Marigold in the bathroom. M.J. fell on his daddy, giggling. From that point the two proceeded to scramble the covers, until Marigold came into the room, toothbrush in hand, watching the wrestling going on. "Don't tear the sheets, guys, we only have one set for that bed since we went to King size." Shaking her head she returned to the sink, mumbling. "They didn't even hear me." It was

Matt tired down first. She heard the cartoons come on. Then Matt was coming through the door.

"I think he missed me," Matt's smile was ear to ear. "I missed him and the misses," he said as his arms went around her. "I can't do this farming bit with you and him here and me there. Something's got to give." He glanced at the clock. "Oh, man, are we gonna' be late for service?"

"Your clothes are hanging on the door. My make-up is on, all I have to do is slip on my mu-mu," she grinned at his questioning look, "well it's either the dress as big as a mu-mu or wear the bed sheet. I think I'm about to pop."

"That brings us to the condition of your feet." He stooped to examine them. "Whatever Mark gave you it seems to be working. Do you feel better?" His expression caused Marigold a nervous laugh.

"Are they that bad? I weighed and I've lost seven pounds of fluid. No wonder I was so sluggish and wanted to sleep."

"I know, Babe," he stalled, finally to ask, "are you up to church?"

"I wouldn't miss showing you off for the world, Farm Boy."

She went willingly into his arms. "I just want to hold you, Tinkerbell," he whispered. "Sometimes I get so worried when I can't see how you are day to day and it comes into my mind that I could lose you."

Drawing back she placed her hands on each side of his face and kissed him, tears in her eyes matched his, "Not if I can help it, Farm Boy. We've sacrificed our time together for you to help your parents, but it has only made us realize what we have. I'll follow the doctor's orders, but promise me, when Harriet calls you'll come straight home." Her expression was serious. "Promise you will."

They were getting out of the van when Marigold saw Andrew and Anne going inside. "Matt, do you remember Andrew's friend, the one who helped him through his stay in jail when Walden pressed charges?"

"The one with the funny name?"

"Yes. Well, Andrew convinced him he needs to be in church. He has attended a few Sundays and had dinner with the group afterwards. Just in case you forgot…his nick name is Pookie. I have no idea his real name."

"He's a different nationality, if I recall." Matt pulled a sleeping M.J. from his car seat. "Spanish?

"Yes, Italian or Spanish…I don't think anyone ever said. It doesn't matter, does it."

"Not to me." Matt grinned. "Me Farm boy, you Tinkerbell. Top that." They entered laughing.

Joe pumped his hand. "Brother it's good to see you."

"Then prove it," Matt said, lifting him off the floor in a bear hug.

"Come on, Matt," Joe's face was turning red. "Don't let Mrs. Powers see you doing this. I'll never live it down." He glanced cautiously to see who witnessed the moment, as Matt sit him down. "We will take this up later," Joe said, wiping his forehead. "That is so embarrassing."

Matt tapped him on the shoulder, "It's love, brother, love. Now preach a good one."

The group filed in, everyone happy to see Matt by Marigold's side. Ellen was guiding the twins to the Nursery, while Matt was following with M.J. still asleep on his shoulder. "Too much wrestling in bed this morning," Matt explained. "How are you Ellen? How's the treatment going?"

"I'm happy to say the treatment is finished and I seem to be regaining energy…which I certainly need."

They returned to find Anne and Andrew with little Andy seated by Ruthie and Andrew's friend settling in next to them. The group had filled two pews. Pastor Joe was beaming as he stepped behind the pulpit. "Welcome. Welcome. To our visitors, our members, to all who love the Lord. Please stand, if you are able and let us sing praise to the Lord, and if there's someone you want to greet, do not stifle the spirit."

The songs spoke to Matt's heart; it was as if he had been dry and barren, his soul seeking.

"This morning our reading is number ninety in the hymnal or you may read the words from the screen. "Hear O Israel: The Lord our God is one Lord." Pastor Joe began and the people answered, "And thou shalt love the Lord thy God with all thine heart and with all thy soul and with all thy might. And these words which I command thee this day, shall be in thine heart."

Matt's heart stirred as he listened. He had missed this; his heart recognized the Holy Spirit working through the words of scripture. "Put on therefore, as the elect of God, kindness, humbleness of mind, meekness, longsuffering." Forbearing one another and forgiving one another, Joe countered and the people replied, "And above all these things put on love which is the bond of perfectness." And let the peace of God rule in your hearts and be ye thankful. "And whatsoever ye do in word or deed, do all in the name of the Lord Jesus, giving thanks to God and the Father by him."

There were so many emotions going on in Matt, it was as if his very being had opened up to the word. "We cannot allow ourselves to hold a grudge when God has written we are to forbear and forgive one another," Pastor Joe was saying. "We cannot speak hateful words and judge others when His word has said we are to be kind to one another, humble, meek and longsuffering when someone makes a mistake. God allows people to be put in our midst that we are to help, sometimes to forgive." He came down from the podium, "Forgiveness is often a hard task. Something we had rather let the other person do, because we just aren't ready. We say they aren't deserving. We hold their sin to our chest while committing our own sin. What was the command? Above all things put on love which is the bond of perfectness. The next words are a blessing. Let the peace of God rule in your heart."

"You want peace in your heart? Do you know Him? In this hour, has the Holy Spirit convicted you of your failure in just one of these gifts of love a Christian has toward another? Has the Holy Spirit whispered you need Him, the one who brings peace and calm in the midst of suffering and trouble? If you do not know Him, now is the time. Jesus said; Let not your heart be troubled, you believe in God, believe also in me."

* * * * * *

Lunch with the group was balm to Matt's soul. "I miss everyone, Marigold," he said, "do you understand?" She saw his misery. She wanted to say come home, Matt but she knew he had to finish this harvest. "I have to leave this afternoon." She understood. He had come home to take care of his wife but he could not take his wife back with him. If his mother had her way she would never be welcome.

"Church was good," she said. "Were you surprised to see Pookie there?"

He scratched his chin, thinking. "I was. What's this I hear about him getting married?

"I don't know," Marigold shook her head. "I hadn't heard that, only that he was dating someone."

"He hasn't brought her to church?"

"Not that I know," Marigold tilt her head. "But I probably wouldn't know who he is dating."

Matt left that afternoon. Marigold fought the urge to cry. "Why am I so emotional," she asked M.J. but he only smiled and pat her shoulder. "Daddy's gone," she stifled a sob building in her throat. "Gone."

Down in spirit she tried to play with M.J., but he was tired from church and taking a nap. She was relieved when the call came in from Matt. "I forgot to tell you Tinker Bell, Walden has escaped. We were never in contact with him but Andrew and Anne certainly were, and as I understand, Walden's in a mood. If he shows up in the Cape, be careful. His reputation precedes him and now that he's stolen some item from the government he says will make the Cape take notice, the law will be after him."

"I overheard Daniel when he took that call at lunch, I heard him ask, "what do you mean an item belonging to the Government that could affect the lives of both of our communities," and on the last he said, "just what we need, one more problem in our group to worry about. Walden intends to hit on us one and all."

"Yeah, Dan and Andrew and I had a few minutes discussion on Walden. This is pretty much the worst, when you get the Feds after you and they've moved two or three into our neck of the woods. Got to go Babe, I've reached the fields and have a bit of work to do before it gets dark. I love you, Tinkerbell."

Chapter Eight

Andrew finished adhering the letters of the law firm onto the glass door. "Well, he said, "now you've experienced all the group together. Do you feel any better about us? You thought we were …"

"Stuck up snobs," Pookie offered. "Well, you were once upon a time. You treated your wife terrible. I don't know about those other guys but I like the women and surprise surprise I like your pastor."

"If you need to talk about yesterday's sermon, I'm game."

"You wantin' to save my soul, white boy?"

Andrew groaned. "Why do you say that, in fact, why do you act like you're the poor chimney sweep and the rest of us are the rich masters. Has anyone behaved that way in the short time you've known us?" Pookie glared at him. "Whether you agree or not," Andrew said,

"The people in the group are some of the best folks you will ever be blessed to know. We stand together. Man. You're a hard case."

* * * * * * *

In the weeks to follow, Pookie did not hide the fact that his courtship of Britany was in full swing. "Man," he'd say, "She's a handful. Did you know about Walden giving her drugs last year?"

"I don't think he forced them on her."

"Oh, that's low. You don't like her at all, do you?"

Andrew thought for a moment how Britany tried to destroy Matt and Marigold's marriage. "I don't like her ethics," he replied. "She has none when it comes to getting what she wants."

"She says she attends church. I thought that was high in your priorities." Hand on hip, Pookie stood firmly rooted, waiting for Andrew's reply. "Well, does it count, or not?"

"It counts because while she is attending, maybe something will speak to her heart and make a difference. As far as that's concerned, maybe your attending will do the same for you."

"I don't get you. You have one set of rules for me. You keep nagging me to come to church with you, but this beautiful young woman attends and you shoot her down. There has to be a reason."

"Don't ask me to supply you with info on your lady. Ask her. It will be interesting to hear what she says and now that Walden is running with the law on his tail, I'd put my money on his return here."

"She's ready to settle down." Pookie said the words so low, Andrew ask him to repeat what he just said. "She's ready to settle down." Pookie made himself look Andrew in the eye. "We got too many years of friendship between us to have a problem over someone I may be considering marriage."

"What?" Andrew pushed away from the desk. Oldham and Winters could wait. "Let me hear you say that again. Aren't you moving a little fast?"

"What's fast about it? She's ready. I'm ready. I want to make her mine."

"And what does the lady say?" Andrew moved a bottle of window cleaner and cloth off the desk.

"She proposed." Pookie picked up the cleaner and attacked the window with a vengeance.

Placing his hands firmly on the desk top, Andrew stared at Pookie. "You know, Buddy, I've been with you through drugs, hiding from the law, and studying together to open this very office…but this, this I cannot believe." He was silent a moment then asked, "Is she pregnant?"

Pookie started to speak, sputtered and threw the cloth on the floor. "We haven't been together that long…besides we've been using Christian guidelines since we've been dating. You take the cake!"

"I'm sorry," he was genuinely sorry to point out his misgivings about Britany James. He reached across to touch Pookie, but Pookie shrugged and pulled away. "I'm sorry, Buddy. I won't do it again."

"For your information, not that it matters, we haven't been together in a Biblical way."

"Like you said, it's none of my business. Just give it a lot of thought, will you? Go slow."

"I already have. I gave her a ring. I'm surprised you'd give me advice."

He needed to work off the angst he was feeling over Pookie's news. Two hours later he closed the blinds, threw the cleaning cloths in the wastepaper can, locked the door and headed home. What Pookie said was true. Pookie had been there when he chased every skirt that appeared promising and drug Anne through financial ruin, while taking their son away from her. Why she ever considered taking him back no one knew. Now they were discussing having another baby and selfishly he knew it was all for him to prove he could be a good husband and father. If the Lord forgave him, why was he still bent on proving himself? Anne deserved better. In his better moments he wondered if her body could stand to carry another baby nine months. He was so deep in thought the ride home was barely noticeable and he failed to make the customary call home to Anne. Once the move was completed to the new office he would let the satellite office go. It was the Judge set him up in it. It was the Judge and Harper straightened him out. Now it was as if he was the daddy figure to Pookie, afraid where Pookie's decision would lead him.

He was relieved Andy was visiting with Harriet. Placing the silverware beside the plates he sit down and waited for Anne. Silent the whole time she was dishing food into their plates he only nodded his like.

"You are awfully quiet," she said. "Is there something wrong I should know about?"

"Pookie is getting married." She glanced up quickly. As if it were his fault he said, "Britany James."

"Britany James? The Britany James?" Andrew nodded. Watching as she folded her napkin and lay it beside her plate. "Are you sure?" She gave a nervous laugh. "I didn't know they knew each other."

He told her about the stop to help someone in trouble, the thank you note and the evolving courtship.

"That can't be very long, Andrew. Has he lost his mind?"

"She ask him to marry her. He has really fallen for her and she is…"

"Beautiful." Anne rose from the table. "For some reason I'm not hungry anymore."

"I know." Andrew leaned over his plate; face down his head in his hands. "I've thought about this, since he left the office, my driving home and I know God is impressing on me that we must do the right thing…you know I was no saint." He lift his eyes to her, pleading in his voice, sadness in his eyes. "Why…Anne, how could you take me back after all the horrible things I did to you?"

"You changed, Andrew, but not one of us will trust her." She began to stack the dishes. "I'm not hungry anymore."

"We can eat left overs tomorrow night." He stared at the bowls of food. "But what do you mean?"

Anne's thoughts were on Andrew's friend. "He's already saved and baptized," she said. "That's one thing, the way she acts another. You and Pookie have become quite close and the group has accepted him, but the women won't trust her and really Andrew… will the men trust themselves if she starts…I'm at a loss for words."

"You mean if she starts playing up to the men."

"I guess." Suddenly, Anne shot straight up. "Andrew, they would be in the same room with Matt and Marigold and you know she has no …no…nothing restrains her. She goes after what she wants."

"And she wants Matthew Langley," Andrew said softly. "Maybe that's what she's doing."

At the Cape

Daniel handed a bundle of bulletins to Father Joe. "Looks like a bumper Sunday," he said, glancing toward the baptistery, "Might even put that to use." He grinned, "I bet you think of Pastor Levi's problem when the heater they used to heat the baptistery water caused a fire that burn them out, I believe at the time you said, if it would bring Walden into the church you'd carry water to fill the baptistery. I believe you said a bit more…." Daniel was enjoying himself. "What was that you said…?"

"Yeah," Joe looked him in the eye, "but I'd do it if it meant Walden and his family would attend, and Ray's family too. Those girls are exposed to, too much worldly business, they need God's love."

Daniel gave him a swift jab in the ribcage knowing what they'd said on the green, forgetting Ray was there with her people, in spirit of course. "Might have to watch what you say, Reverend, it could bite you in the rear." Ray's family was a bone of contention with some of the congregation's members.

"All right, so I said I'd preach standing half naked in the rain if anyone could get Ray Morning and her girls in church and I did make a statement of sorts about Walden when….let me see…." No doubt they secretly shared the thought that a church should always have people of controversy, like Ray. That was what church was for, wasn't it? If only the righteous attended, the work was not being done.

"Uh, Hum," Daniel was shaking his head, his hand out, fingers moving." Come on. What else did you say?" Now he started laughing. "Don't deny it; you said if someone could get Walden saved it would save the Cape in the long run and by the way, the Feds think he is headed our way."

"Walden with all his endeavors." Shaking his head, Joe knew when he was defeated. "Why do you remember the most mundane things? As I recall we were blustering, trying to outdo each other."

"Well, it's October, the farmers don't want rain, but if it does, I'll pick you up and take you down town where the statue stands in the center of the street and you can preach your heart out. I'll even call the newspaper so they can cover it."

"You wouldn't."

Dan was writing on an invisible wall. "Local pastor makes good on his word. Standing half naked in the rain, he offers the word and love of God to every man, regardless of color or creed. Come one, come all."

"You would." He grabbed Daniel's arm, the two were immediately in combative hold. "Yes, you would and you would be right there by me, wouldn't you?"

"Yes sir." Pulling back, straightening his shirt, Daniel thought maybe it was time he warned the Reverend. "Gotta tell you something, Father Joe."

"Lord have mercy," Joe replied. "When you call me father, I know it's riveting because I'm not a father."

"It's something coming in from the grapevine. You remember that young lady wearing the bright blue dress you ask me who she was when we were at Newhaven and you were preaching revival."

"You said her parents were killed in an accident and that she was the one tried to break up Matt and Marigold." He grinned. "You finally told me her name was Britany James. Am I right?"

"Yes, she tried to break them up after they were married and had M.J."

"What does that have to do with me or Christ Church?" Joe sit on the front pew staring at the stained glass window behind the podium. "That scene of Christ kneeling in the garden gives me such peace. It was there he prayed not my will but thine. He had ask his heavenly father to remove the cup of his dying on the cross but realized he must give his life as atonement, for our sins, Daniel, for us."

"I know." Reverence brought Daniel closer, where he sat by Joe, their knees touching. "Do we need to pray, a prayer of thanksgiving?"

"We will, but first, what was the grapevine's buzz?"

"You know Andrew's friend has recently started attending worship hour, with us?"

"Yes." Puzzled, Joe studied Daniel. "I'm waiting for a clue to connect Pookie and Miss James."

"They are getting married."

"Is there a reason we should object? Has she or Pookie, well, is there something I don't know?"

"No. Not that I know of. Are you surprised?"

"I think I've reached a stage not much surprises me but…I wasn't aware they knew each other." He studied Daniel. "What does their getting married have to do with me or Christ Church?" Pacing a bit, Joe finally sank onto the front pew, sitting there staring at the stained glass window. "You know Jesus prayed not my will but thine be done and that's what we have to do. Jesus was talking to his heavenly father; He ask from a human heart that was saddened at Judas betrayal and a human body that would be wracked with pain as they tried to kill him. His Heavenly Father loved him but he could not remove the cup of his dying on the cross, and Jesus realized he must give his life as atonement for our sin. He did that for us." He drew a deep breath. "This is important or you wouldn't be telling me. There's something about Britany James and her young man…?"

Daniel shook his head, "it seems a mystery. If you remember at the hospital she and Herm Smith were holding hands and now from Andrew I hear this piece of news, because of Pookie being his partner."

"So you are giving me fair warning. But Miss James is a member at Shining Light Church, isn't she?"

"Honestly, I don't know." Daniel stood. "I'm headed home, reverend, just stopped to check on you."

"Just stopped to rattle my chain," the reverend muttered. "Now I gotta deal with May and the girls."

Daniel's laughter rang through the hall on his way out. He hoped Ellen and Ruthie would have returned from Newhaven, *but* his aunt was there, baking cookies. "What a surprise," they were hugging like lost friends. "When did you get back from your trip?"

Georgia waved a jeweled hand in the air. "Today, and came right over to see the children." She sighed. "Of course the new sitter was here; I called Ellen and ask if I could spend time with them." Georgia laughed. "Of course she couldn't turn me down and I then sent the sitter home and had them all to myself." She saw the look on his face. "You think they are too much for me?" She doubled over laughing. "Remember Rosie went with me and two other gals, well, I couldn't leave Rosie at the wharf could I?"

Daniel looked around. "Rosie is here?" Georgia was pointing toward the bedrooms.

"No grandkids, there, either, so when I say I'm coming to see the twins, she comes too."

Daniel was in the hall, by now, calling her name. All he heard was a loud *shhh*. There on Danny's bed was Rosie, Sammy, Danny, Holly and Noel, all asleep except Rosie, who was waving and smiling. He put out a hand and pulled her up. Once in the hall, he hugged her and whispered, "If you weren't so little you couldn't pull that off." To his aunt he said, "Did you see that? All of them sound asleep on one bed."

"I bet you want to know how that happened." Rosie was still smiling. "I read to them, ten stories."

"Thank goodness," Daniel slapped his forehead. "I was afraid you drugged them. That doesn't happen often." He was eyeing Rosie, his mouth drawn at the corners. "But that's almost hard to believe."

"Not if you take into account, we crawled through that fake tunnel, did the twist on those gizmos, 'til the kids finally conked out, but I couldn't get up."

"Aunt Georgia, why didn't you help her?"

"I was too tired; those trips through the tunnel are work, that's when I decided I'd bake cookies."

He shook his head. "You two are the strangest old girls I've ever known."

"Don't tell Ellen, she might not let us do this again."

"Do what again?" Ellen and Ruthie were coming through the door. Squealing, Ruthie was hugging Georgia and then passed over to Rosie. Ellen's smile brightened. "Wish I was loved like that." She reached for a cookie. "Umm, Aunt Georgia, we sure do need your lovin' care."

"Then wash up, peeps," Aunt Georgia said. "Dinner is in the oven. A casserole you won't forget."

"How was the trip to Newhaven?" Daniel was helping Ellen fill the glasses. "Did you take the hat?"

"The trip was good and we did take the hat to her. She seemed quiet, I thought, did you, Ruthie?"

"She's worried," Ruthie replied. She and her mother exchanged looks. "I'll tell you later."

"And you saw Mrs. Merkal?" Daniel glanced at Ellen. "It's not time for the baby, yet, is it?"

Ruthie laughed, "Not until the tulips bloom." Her laugh was infectious. "Is that good, or what?"

"It's good, Ruthie," Daniel said, smiling. "I bet you were the cutest one ever but I didn't get to see you." He reached across to hold her hand. "Shall we say grace? "Heavenly Father, we thank you for this day, for each other and time together. Now we ask your blessing on this food that we might use it to our bodies and to your glory. Thank you for our family and Aunt Georgia and Rosie. Amen."

The casserole was served with fresh salad and Aunt Georgia's cookies for dessert. "We need to talk about the ball, its next week end, remember?" She smiled at Ellen. "Remember your first one, Ellen? You wore that red off shoulder gown and Bitty was all dolled up in blue." She turned to Rosie. "You were there, it was a good ball until Andrew Graves showed up drunk and ripped his ex-wife's, gown from her body." Glancing Ruthie's way, she added, "She was mortified, we all were. Sorry, Ruthie, but life is ugly sometimes. For a while that night we had an ugly spell because of Andrew Graves."

"Well, Aunt Georgia, everything's in order, the invitations go out this coming Monday; The hotel staff begins decorating and all you have to do is sign your name on all receipts. How does that sound?"

"Expensive," Georgia replied. "But it's worth it, we turn the donations in to our favorite charity and feel better for the effort required to make the ball work."

Chapter Nine

Newhaven

Suze stopped in to check on Mabel. "You weren't in church, yesterday," she said as Mabel took the chair opposite at the table. "I was concerned. You know the flu or some kind of virus is going around."

"All I have is a head full of blubber," Mabel replied. "Nate was worried over Britany. I do believe we drove four hundred miles. But, no, we didn't find her, and then this morning she walked back in." There was a sound as both heads turned and Britany was coming into the room.

"Hey, how you two doing?" Britany slipped into the third chair as if the three met daily. "I need a little advice." She opened her phone to photos. "Look at these pictures, if you will and tell me if you think there's one good enough to use in the newspaper."

"Who is this guy, your date to the ball?" Mabel glanced up from studying the picture of the two. "Look, here, Suze this is a good one. What do you think? The one he's standing behind her or the one facing each other."

"They remind me of wedding photos." Suze caught Britany's eye. "Are they wedding pictures?"

Britany shook her head. "No, we want a good one for the newspaper to announce our engagement."

"Engagement?" The two voices sounded surprised but elated reacting to the word. "So that's what you've been doing when you left and didn't tell us where you were going." Mabel asked, relieved.

"You have been kind in that regard," Britany replied. "Usually I was just starting my day with the sunrise down by the river." She laid the photos on the table. "My life is not what it used to be."

"So who is the lucky fellow?" Mabel was beaming. Suddenly this girl was her responsibility. "Will he give you a ring? When is the date?" Mabel reached across to hug a very restrained and cool Britany who was now displaying a solitary diamond on the second finger of her left hand. In a minutes time Suze and Mabel were bent over studying not only the picture of the couple but the perfect diamond. Perhaps now things would liven up around the place. Surely the fellow's family would have a say. "I don't know him," Suze said. "Do you Mabel? But we still want to meet him." Suze finished, "You must be the happiest girl in the world." Britany made no reply. She was wearing her mother's ring.

* * * * * * * *

He watched from a distance. She said her stay with the old lady was coming to an end. If she didn't mess up, she would be on her own again. He wasn't certain if that was a good thing or not. She'd made a lot of mistakes during the time he had her on the drugs. It seemed her upbringing had been stable and strong due to being born to older parents. True, he caught her at her most vulnerable, when her parents died, when she couldn't sleep and her nerves were on edge. His kind fatherly way, said, "young lady, I would never recommend you take any drug that would bring harm. That's part of the oath, that life is a precious gift and we must treat it as such." Two weeks of the drug and she was hooked. Before long, he had her eating out of his hand, but then the day in the park broke the ring, scattered his dealers and nearly took his life. He would never forget seeing her laying under that table, when they found her, shaking and afraid. They, meaning Matt Langley and his wife, got to her before he could.

The irony was, they both ended up in the same hospital, along with his cousin, Herman Smith. He thought he had made it to safety when they found him. The rich old biddy, Harriet Becker's maid had lowered him with an iron skillet all right, but at the hospital checking him in, he found a way out. Now, it was his lot to leave his maneuverings to the dark of night. He was taking a chance following her today but he needed to know if he could trust her. She refused the drugs, saying they confused her mind and due to her health she could no long take them. She was firm. No need arguing with her, instead in order to manipulate her he became her dear friend. He wanted to laugh but someone might hear. He learned the hard way; he was no one's friend.

She was coming out, carrying a large suitcase, using her foot to close the door. She struggled a bit hoisting the suitcase into the truck, but he couldn't help her. She had to make it on her own. He followed when she pulled out into the street. It would be interesting to see if she was going home or staying in the Cape over the weekend. His mind was not set on her loyalty to him. It had been but now she had been under the influence of Mabel Hisaw, a Christian old biddy if he'd ever seen one. He had overheard her talking in class, during the time he was posing as Herm, "I think we have to try to live according to the Ten Commandments, and remember Jesus said, we are to love our neighbor." Mabel Hisaw smiled while he grit his teeth. As for Herm, he had tied him to the post at that old farm house and left him to die a slow death. Now he laughed, his head thrown back as he enjoyed the sound. Diabolical, Britany had called it. Diabolical.

Trailing two car lengths behind, he followed her into the Cape, his interest peaked when she pulled into an empty space in front of one of the law firms. It amazed him; they had boarded up his place. They had no idea he was still around. A master at disguise, he walked in and out of their lives, listening and filing information away until it was needed. What kind of name was that on the door? Pookie? What?

A young man came out of the building headed toward Britany's car and climbed in. He saw the man lean to kiss her and suddenly his rage erupted. Had he wasted a morning watching her and this was the reward? She was his. He'd made certain of that. Her car pulled away from the curb and sped down the street. He was angry, the vehicle he was driving wasn't responding. He backed into someone's car, pulled forward and rammed the one in front, then he was free, his vehicle out on the street. But where did they go?

Britany and Pookie

"You were mysterious, when you called, saying we were going on a ride through the country. Where are we going?"

Britany laughed. "Don't you trust me?" She watched his expression change. "Don't be alarmed. We are going to my childhood home. How does that sound?"

"There's a reason?" Pookie settled back in the seat as she nodded. "I just as well enjoy the ride."

"One of the things I like about you is the way you accept things easily, and that mellow voice soothes."

He grinned. "That's two things. So you like my voice. Well, how nice, Miss Britany, I appreciate it."

"You got the Southern boy stuff down to a T." Her eyes were beginning to sparkle. "I need your advice on something." He seemed to sit up straighter. "If we marry in one of the churches, we have to decide which, but if it is at Applegate, then there are a few minor repairs to make. Do you have a preference?"

"No, you let me know and if I can help with the repairs, I will." She told him about the farm's name, how her parent's died and with the small talk, they were soon turning into the drive. The house sit directly before them, two storied, tall columns, a bit dusty but it was the year for such upheaval. She was studying the upper windows, a ladder stretching within three feet. "I see something up there," she pointed, "that last windstorm I bet."

Inside, a worker was tidying up where his lunch had been in a crumbled sack. "Miss Britany," he exclaimed. "We're glad you could come back today. The roofer will be here at two and then the brick layer for the fountain's foundation where the old oak fell on it. Til then, I have a few more task." He excused himself and was gone.

"Come on, for our little excursion around the farm we'll take the gator." Pookie saw, this was the part she liked. If he was guessing, she had been raised a tom boy. Wiping the seat clean, they climbed in and the tour began. "There," she said, pointing "is where the apple orchard used to be. The trees are long since gone and we farm the area, but there's an occasional wild tree with very sharp green apple."

"This is a lot to take in," Pookie was shaking his head. "May I ask why did you choose me, to marry?"

She pulled beneath an old oak tree, cut the engine and stared at him. "I guess if I were you, I'd want to know too." She sighed. "It's only fair to you; you will take a lot of flak, marrying me. When you came to my apartment I was relieved you were tall, handsome and intelligent, but your kindness sold me on you. You didn't actually apply for the job, I got you there on false pretense, but I chose you."

"I don't recall any extra effort on my part. A beautiful woman, a need to share something with me; I assumed it was a legal matter since you went through the office. I was sold on whatever the project was, but a proposal of marriage…that was some big deal." He whistled Dixie to make his point.

"You've seen the house. Now what do you think about being married here rather than a church."

"You're smiling. Do you like my old homestead?" Her own smile widened. "So do I, I think we can pull this off in two weeks, don't you?" Her hand was on the key to the ignition. "I'll have the roof repaired, the foundation to the fountain finished by then. Are there things we need to discuss on your part? Your schedule?"

"I'll check with my partner." Pookie was rubbing his hands together, as he often did when thinking. "Can I ask, what kind of wedding are you planning?"

"The wedding of the year. I'll order your tux; go into the next state to find my dress." She grinned mischievously, "I think a grand poufy deal will look nice with this place, what do you think?" She tilt her head just so, a coy expression on her face, "do you want to back out? Tell me before I buy the dress."

"Not back out, that's not what I'm thinking. If you plan a big wedding, I suppose that means your family, mine, your neighbors, who I work with, just thinking and its mind boggling for someone like me."

"Exactly." She replied. "Who is your boss?"

"Andrew Graves. His wife is Anne."

"Sounds familiar but I can't place him. I have enemies, you know?" Their eyes met. "I do."

"Is that why you needed a man? Me?"

"No." She revved up the engine and they shot across the pasture toward the house. Suddenly she was tense and foreboding. He ask no questions and she offered nothing more. He had all the information he needed.

She met with the repairmen, then the guy they first encountered. "Sam, if you need help, then find someone. In two weeks I want the house washed down, have the fountain running, and there between the two great oaks after the lawn is mowed, shrubbery trimmed and all debris removed, there have the people who will be bringing chairs do their sitting up. Let's say the day previous the ceremony."

"What are you planning, if I may ask?"

"I'm getting married, Sam." She smiled. "It's going to be good. All the sadness we've known, the dreariness of Applegate, will disappear in time. You all are invited…but be sure to tell Kasandra and Olivia someone has to help with the caterer. She will take care of the food products, but someone should be available that knows where to find the items she needs."

When she handed Sam a list, Pookie began to think she had been planning for months. As they started the trip back to the Cape, he asked, "Shall I give you a ring?"

"Of course," a different expression came into her face, he wasn't certain if she was projecting happiness or calculating the effect the ring would have on others. "I've not experienced a ring or gift of any significance in quite a while. Now, tell me about your friends, who you wish to invite. Name them off and give me a list when you can, say tomorrow evening."

Pookie whistled. "Lady, once you get going you don't stop, do you?" More plans had been made this afternoon than a month of Monday's at the office. "I have a question," he said. "Do you plan for me to be present? No, my question really is, must I lose the pony tail. I want to keep it."

She studied his features. "No, it gives you character. Keep the pony tail." She seemed hesitant for a moment, and then said, "We will be attending Hutson's ball, too, so you will need your first tux for it."

He was stunned. "I've never attend a ball. Are you sure about this? It's for the elite."

"It's a fund raiser. Our money is good. They can use it." Her lips formed a straight line. "We're going."

They were silent on the trip home. Other than inquiring as to his shirt and pant size, she had very little to say. "You wear what size jacket," she asked. He replied, and then list it on her notes. She let Pookie out at his office and headed back to Mable Hisaw's home. Tomorrow she would go into Tennessee to purchase her wedding dress.

The call came through around nine o'clock. It was Britany. "I didn't think to ask. What is your real name?"

Pookie thought of all the names he had used. Silently he scrolled the list in his memory, what would she want? Then, he decided to give her the one most likely. In truth, his mother had let him slide through the cracks; Pookie, they called him, as an infant and it stuck. There were three men he respected; everyone called them by their last name. Then there was the name his mother seemed to worry over. Perhaps he was the one, his father, he had never known. Sometimes the teachers called him George, he wondered why other than there was a picture of George Washington on the wall in each teachers room. "You do have a name?" She was waiting."

"Edwardo Fernandez. George Edwardo Fernandez." The names rolled off his tongue; there was a melody to his name. Yes, that's who he was. There was no one to challenge it. He would make it legal.

* * * * * * *

The invitations arrived the following Tuesday. She had wasted no time. What was the rule, at least two weeks before ceremony?

Britany James and George Edward Fernandez request the honor of your presence at Applegate Farm. The date and time followed. In all, Britany sent out two hundred invitations, she expected two dozen would be fair attendance, but she prepared as though the whole world would celebrate with her and Pookie. As soon as they were married he would be George Edward, unless he preferred Edward. She smiled. Life was moving along. She could only guess the reaction of some folk receiving the invitation.

The same day she mailed the invitations, she ordered the cake, contacted the catering service and drove to Memphis to find her wedding dress. Rather than break tradition, she did not ask Pookie's attendance, instead she invited Miss Mabel Hisaw and Mrs. Suze Norman to accompany her.

They were all excited. "On the day your wedding invitation arrived, we also received an invitation to attend the Hutson Ball at the Cape. Usually the ones receiving those are the city officials but we suspect Mr. Dan and Miss Ellen leading our revival music may be the reason, but we don't have festive wear for a ball. Pastor Levi and Leah received invites too." When Britany didn't reply, Mabel took cue and closed the subject. The miles passed with talk of wedding preparation and then they were at the Bridal Shoppe.

When by coincidence Britany found two dresses that fit perfect and gave her the feeling of being a bride, she eyed Mrs. Norman finding them near the same size. "Would you please try on the second dress and stand by me that I might study in the mirror which one I like best?" Today she would forsake pride and ask. "Please Mrs. Suze." The dress was a task she must finish this trip.

Reluctantly Suze agreed and the attendant offered assistance as the poufy gown was slipped over her head, beautiful jewelry accessories and a veil were added. Suze, was a beautiful bride in standing.

"You both take my breath away," Mabel exclaimed. "Suze you are quite lovely and Britany, all heads will turn when you walk to your beloved. Oh, my, thank you for asking us to come with you. What a delight."

"You both must find a dress. My treat," Britany said. "No, don't start protesting. I want to do this. Can you imagine how sad it would have been for me to come alone with no one's support or encouragement?"

"Which do you like best, the one you are wearing or Suze's? All those hand sewn pearls, the lace, I love it but the one you are wearing, fits your figure; it is high end, I would not want to have your task in deciding." Mabel walked around them admiring the silken creations they wore.

"I think it comes down to color," Britany replied. "The more creamy aged white compliments my skin tones, whereas the pure white makes me appear washed out. But Suze with her olive skin can wear either; still the white does not have the effect on her it does on me. Do you see what I mean? She wears the white very well."

"They are both the very essence of romance. My goodness," Mabel was ecstatic, "Who knew what a woman needed to look good?" They all laughed.

"All right," Britany said, "First we take off the dresses and then find one for each of you. Any idea of the color you want?"

"I saw a beautiful lilac," Mabel gave a soft self-conscious clearing of the throat. "I can pay for it."

"No, you can't. How about you, Suze? I saw you studying that blue lace. Is that the one?"

"Oh, Britany," Mabel's voice was almost reverent. "This is the most beautiful dress I've ever worn."

"You do look good," Britany took a strand of pearls off the nearby table and fastened it around Mabel's neck. "Perfect, do you have pearls at home?"

"The blue dress is too large," Suze said. Without a word Britany hand in to Suze a soft apricot and an ecru of the same style.

"I saw it was a twelve and knew it was way too large for you. Try one of those and see if you like it."

Suze tried both, showing them each time. "Now it's a hard decision. They're both pretty. What do you think?"

"The ecru," Mabel and Britany said in unison. "It leans more toward taupe, a year round color and looks great." For accessories, Britany showed her a gold chain with a teardrop pearl in the center. "Ladies, we are complete. It has been a good day. I was fortunate to find shoes to match the wedding gown and they gave me a pair of pearl earrings I might wear. I'll know that day." Placing the accessories back in their places, "We're ready to go," she said, "and I am happy we were successful."

Once they were on the road again, Mabel ask, "Where will you live, Britany?"

"I think in time, at the farm, but for now, this year anyway, Edward will keep his apartment and we can live there pretty comfortably."

"Well, don't forget us," Mabel said. "I won't. You're family now."

* * * * * * *

It was a busy afternoon in the Cape, particularly at Marigolds. A whole line of jewelry had been brought in for the Hutson Ball. The Shoppe was buzzing. "We are just becoming acquainted with Andrew's friend and now the lady with the reputation will be in our midst." Leaning close to whisper in Anne's ear, Dorothy Harper asked, "How did Marigold take the news?"

"She isn't saying much. This is the woman willing to destroy her marriage."

"Well it had to be a shock. Why would anyone be so obvious, knowing Marigold and Britany's history?"

"For the most part, we don't know. Is this a well thought out plan or, is it two people getting married on short notice asking friends to attend?" Anne's troubled expression matched everyone else's.

"We've only known the groom a very short time and the bride's history with this group isn't good."

Ellen had been listening. "So what is our part in this, to lend support? Possibly the groom's in the dark."

Anne shook her head, "If anyone can pull something worth considering out of it, it would be you."

"Harper feels Andrew has been a great influence on Pookie." Dorothy added, "I noticed on the invitation his name is George Edward." She laughed,"I always hesitate to call him Pookie."

"Generally speaking," Anne asked, "Ellen, are you saying it is the Christian thing to do for Pookie?"

"He's Andrew's partner in the law firm, won't Andrew support him?" Anne nodded yes. "Then as a group, we have a lot of thinking to do on this. We suspect it isn't easy for Marigold but Britany is Matt's childhood friend. They are all caught in the middle; we are just the outside fringe. We want to show loyalty to Marigold because Britany hurt her many times, but we have to pray Britany has changed. She was in with the worst when Walden had hold on her. Who knows what Walden is plotting, being the evasive master mind he is but prayer changes things. We can pray something good comes out of it."

"This means we are going to attend the wedding, right? "Anne closed her eyes a second, "You know Pookie ask Andrew to be his best man." She sighed. "How could he turn down his partner?"

"Oh, the web we weave," Dorothy quoted, "When first we practice to deceive."

* * * * * * *

"I hear there was a little meeting of the minds at Marigold's this afternoon."

Ellen glanced up from writing a check to the phone company. "How would you know that?"

"Andrew called me; he is upset over the whole thing. He's afraid Pookie is making a mistake, the man has fallen head over heels in love with the woman and thinks she hung the moon."

"You know what?" Ellen sealed the envelope. "I can't dwell on Pookie's wedding with the Hutson Ball this weekend and your aunt wants to bring the twins in to show them off, so we have shoes to polish, outfits to match to assemble, not to mention your wifey hasn't tried on her dress to be sure it fits."

"My wifey would be beautiful in a burlap sack." Daniel came behind her, wrapped his arms around her shoulders and leaned down to kiss her. "So you think Andrew's worrying is useless? I told him that, too."

"Consider the fowl of the air, our heavenly Father takes care of them, won't he take care of us?"

"I agree." Daniel pecked a kiss on her cheek. "Did Aunt Georgia say anything to you about us singing a few songs with the orchestra?" He grinned. "You know, to bring back our first Hutson Ball memory when we not only sang but put our best foot forward dancing as Fred and Ginger. She said to tell you she loves you and she has already called the sitter to take care of all four of our youngsters."

"Your Aunt Georgia has remarkable energy for a lady her age, what she doesn't have is two sets of twins." She stood up. "Come with me, Buster. Together we will conquer the wardrobe department."

Daniel rubbed his hands together. "Goody. You try on your dress and we'll practice dancing."

"Not on your life, Buster, we are going to polish four pairs of little scuffed up shoes. Isn't that fun?"

Newhaven

"You look very handsome, Nate." Mabel admired Nate in his charcoal gray suite, blue shirt and checked tie of a blue and gray mix. "Who helped assemble your attire?"

Nate grinned, "So you don't think I'm capable of putting together a pair of pants and a shirt?" His eyes twinkled. "Britany found out I was escorting you and Suze and nothing do her but come see what was in my closet." He bowed and reached to take her hand. "I must say you look lovely. I'm wondering, do you dance?"

Mabel blushed. "Actually, it's a lost art for me, early in life we danced but there's no place to dance in Newhaven and we did have that minister that said dancing was a sin of the devil and he better not hear anyone in his congregation was indulging." She laughed. "And there all the time on the front row of our church sit his cousin drunk as a skunk most Sundays, anyway a hangover from the night before."

"That must have been hard to swallow for a minister."

"Don't know if it was or not," Mabel replied. "A person probably won't kill anyone dancing, will they but driving drunk, many a soul here in Newhaven had to get out of that man's way."

"I agree." Nate was glancing at his watch. "Do we drive down to pick up Suze?"

"In about twenty minutes. Let's sit out on the porch until then. It's a nice night."

* * * * * * * *

Suze had seen Nate pass by at the same time she heard the computer receiving. She had tried to break off the calls and texts but he would not allow it. "No, no, my lady," he would play upon her kindness. "We are merely conversing. We have met, my lady, we are friends. I know you have an interest in me as I have in you." When she refused to reply, he would ask, "Why do you fight our friendship, my Suze. It is meant to be." Tonight, she said hello. She always felt guilt that Wade was being left out, forgotten and she had vowed that would never happen. How could she have a relationship, if only friendship, with this man when her heart still ached for Wade? Every minute of every day she remembered Wade; still knowing when the call would come through or the ding of the computer saying he had text, she found herself drawing nigh, and wondering always at his last entry, I send my love on wings of angels. What did he know about angels? Still it was intriguing, as one might send a blessing. But tonight she would experience the ball for the first time; perhaps she could forget him for a while. And then it was time to leave. Suze glanced at her reflection in the mirror, the dress Britany bought for her was beautiful. She looked like a happy person. How could the image of a person be so deceiving? What was a ball if there was no one to enjoy it with?

Chapter Ten

Gates House

"He-he-he-he, Who'se ready to go with me?" Using a rolled up paper for a megaphone Daniel called out to his children. "Come out, come out, wherever you are. Don't be late for Hutson's annual Ball."

Ruthie came running. "I'm here, Daddy. I'm ready." The twins were close behind, dressed in one pieced black velvet rompers, white shirt with bow tie and knee high socks and black shoes.

"Look at my children," Dan's voice was dramatic, the smile on his face genuine. "Look at Miss Ruthie, a plate of fashion in her crème topped black velvet skirted evening dress. We say evening because it's just above the ankle where we see a flash of black hose dipping down into shiny black patent shoes. Oh, yes, Miss Ruthie will draw the attention of every person present at Aunt Georgia's Hutson Ball. None can compare with the twins, Samuel and Daniel in their festive wear, a complimentary match to Miss Ruthie. But wait, there's only one set of twins, I believe two are missing. What will they be wearing? Oh, yes, I see them now. Holly and Noel, dressed in deep burgundy red velvet, a pacifier in each mouth and a white bib tucked beneath their chins. And for now they are not wearing shoes, only knee socks that cover their fat chubby little knees. And where is the Mommie of the brood.... Oh, Mommie.....

Blowing into the paper megaphone, Dan gave his imitation of the opening bugle call used at the race track. Da da da da da daa..... Oh, there she is Missus Ah Gates Ah...there she is...our rising star, she keeps us and feeds us...loves and...."

Ellen gave her best, trying to slink into the room, "Hey Big Boy, are you out of your lovin mind, all those kiddoes there watching you play that paper bugle, and not too good either if I might say so..." By then she was laughing. "I don't have the air for this stuff anymore but I'll give you credit..." She stopped speaking because Daniel was planting a big smooch on her lips.'

"You look gorgeous, Mom-ma. Have I seen that dress before?"

"Only three days ago," she said dryly. "Now, let's load 'em up, cowboy." She stood back to admire her husband. "Lookin' good there, friend. I'll have to watch the women tonight. They'll be linin' up."

Daniel was rubbing his hands together, "I hope so." Then he picked up the double diaper bags, lift Holly onto his shoulder and led the way. "You got Noel, Mom-ma? We're off to the Hutson's Annual Ball."

"Everyone's buckled in. Light on in the house, door shut, garage door down. Count the kids again. One-two-three-four-five. All righty, we can go." Sitting behind the steering wheel, he changed into responsible Dad. "We are gonna have fun, Momma."

"I hope." She met his glance. "Other years have had their drama, but this one, I pray is good."

"What could possibly go wrong?"

"My thoughts, exactly," she replied. "In view of a couple new people attending this year, forgive me, I hope for the best. At least this year your aunt isn't suffering from a broken foot or leg. Knock on wood."

Mabel and Nate at the Ball

"It's all in fun, Mabel," Nate was saying as they entered the building to camera's flashing and a red runner stretching all the way to the dance floor. A young man had stepped up to escort Suze, taking time to pose with her, and then leaving Nate and Mabel in the lime light to seat her at the nearest table.

"Good evening, Mrs. Norman," he said. "Have a wonderful evening and thank you for coming."

They sat watching people arrive, some opting for the red carpet and others, not. Daniel Gates was the Master of Ceremony. "We welcome you," he said, smiling. Our people will try to meet your every need. You have only to ask. First, we have some of our local talent present and then while dinner is being served, our music will continue. The reason we have Hutson's Ball annually began as a means to draw together, as a community dipping into our pockets to make donation to a worthwhile cause and this year we decided to send to the people whose homes have been flooded, people who often need the most unique little item, a comb or brush, things our donations will provide many times over for blankets and pillows, and yes toothbrush and toothpaste; Little and large from your hearts to theirs. Now, thank you for coming let the festivities begin."

The band struck up Jimmy Dorsey music, and several older people rose to go to the dance floor. Dan came for Ellen. "it always helps if we are out there with the others," he explained to several ladies sitting nearby. "You are very welcome to our dance floor."

With that, he and Ellen spun into steps, that would have pleased a professional dancer.

"Your Mommie is beautiful," Anne said, arriving at the table where Ruthie was sitting. "I am watching the door," she explained, "because Andrew is coming later with his friends." When Ruthie waved to Marigold and Matt, she thought she saw Anne visibly stiffen. "Something wrong?" Anne didn't reply.

Georgia Hutson was working the floor, shaking hands with patrons that went back to when the Hotel began, "clean sheets and a clean bathroom," she smiled. "That's what was important then but now we must have Wi-Fi and though we couldn't offer it in our beginning days, we now have a bountiful breakfast."

Hugging Ruthie, she said "Come on back when you want sweetheart, with me and Rosie and the twins."

They were well into the second hour when Andrew arrived with his lawyer friend and a woman Ruthie recognized as the lady Matt and Marigold had rescued off the street when the man in jail escaped. She remembered her mother that morning had said watch her but don't go to her and then when the lady was lying under the table on the street she had been so concerned she had run to tell Marigold to please help her and Matt did. Ruthie turned to tell Anne Andrew was there but Anne had moved on.

Now the woman was looking around. Ruthie thought she didn't know anyone. That was a terrible feeling. Each year at school she felt afraid no one would be there that she knew but they always were. The men were in conversation. Ruthie decided she would go speak to her. She walked around the edge of the dance floor and came up to her side.

"Hello."

Britany stared at the child. She had met this girl before, but where? Now the girl held out her hand. Britany had no choice, she wrapped her own around that smaller hand and it was as if time stood still. Times of her life seemed to flash through her mind. Her mother was brushing her hair and they were laughing about something the clown did at her birthday party. She heard her mother's voice and then the scene switched, she was fishing with her dad. She caught the little sun perch and wanted to take it home to her mother. Shouldn't we let it grow, her daddy asked. His voice was kind. Sixteen. Drivers license, a new car and showing it to Matt. She was happy. Suddenly there were voices. Britany blinked.

"Hi," Ruthie's sweet voice reached the lady above the din of others. "You may not remember me. I am Ellen's daughter. We sit together at Shining Light Church when there was a Lady's meeting."

"I do remember." Britany smiled. "I'm glad you mentioned that, I was trying to recall where I had seen you. We were next to each other in the circle of prayer." The child was smiling and nodding yes. "How are you?"

"I'm fine. Would you like to sit with me?" Ruthie pointed to the other side of the room. "Our group will all be there eventually."

"By saying group, do you think I will know any of your people?"

"My parents, Dan and Ellen, Anne and of course you know Andrew, he's standing right behind you, and then there's Harriet and Andy and Matt and Marigold." She smiled. "There are others."

"Yes, that's plenty. Let me see what Edward and Andrew decide, but thank you, Ruthie."

"Hey Shuga Buga," Andrew stepped forward, "I just recognized you all dressed up, Ruthie." He gave her a hug and a kiss on the cheek. I didn't know you knew Britany. Have you met Pookie, AKA Edward?" The tall guy with the pony tail stepped from behind. Ruthie accepted his hand as Andrew ask, "Ruthie, would you tell Anne I'm here. I'll catch up with her in a minute or two." Ruthie nodded and left.

There were few her age at the Ball. The difference, she supposed was the Ball was a part of Daniel's family background. His Aunt wanted to give the people of the town a gala event. Many looked forward to the Ball as the event of the year. Aunt Georgia had taken Ruthie in as though she were born to the family. Daniel adopted her and she never doubted he loved her as his own. He said he learned how to love when his parents died and his aunt and uncle took him in. "They became my parents,' he explained once to Ruthie, "and in time I became their child. They never rushed me and from them I learned if something is meant to be in time it will happen." Ruthie hoped no one rushed Britany.

The Ball was in full swing when Marigold stepped out on Hutson curb. The valets ask Matt, "Sir do you want us to park your car?" His mind on other things, Matt drove toward parking.

"Either he didn't see or hear you," Marigold said. "But thank you." She walked under the burgundy canopy. "It's sprinkling, now, isn't it?" The valet nodded, opening the door for her and Marigold went inside to wait for Matt.

"Aren't you ravishing?" Andrew had purposely waited for Marigold's arrival. "I need to tell you something." He leaned in to whisper something in her ear. Startled, Marigold straightened the expression on her face difficult to read. "I thought you should hear it coming from me, Marigold."

"Thanks, I guess," she replied, as Matt joined them. "Tell him."

"Pookie is here with Britany, Matt. He accepted the invitation that came to the office and added her."

"Business as usual, huh, Andrew?" Matt shook his head in dismay. "Maybe Britany's better."

"He promised me there would be no problems coming from them, Matt. Hadn't you rather hear from me than be surprised?" Andrew's voice sounded strained, reaching a higher pitch than he intended. "Look, I've been sweating bullets over this. What would you have done?"

Glancing first at his wife and then his friend, Matt offered his hand. "It's all right, Buddy." He gave Andrew a nudge. "Go find your wife and I'll be here with mine. You okay, hon?" Pulling her into the curve of his body, he whispered, "It sucks, but lets you and I meet it as if it doesn't matter. Are you game?" He saw she had turned pale. "You're not going to purge are you? What do I need to do?"

"Let me get this in my mind," she replied. "I'm fine, I just didn't expect her to be here and hopefully we will all act like grownups and have a good evening."

"Thank you, Tinkerbell." His smile was filled with gratitude. "My heart is ten pounds lighter, already." Across the way he saw Nate helping Mabel and her friend find an empty table. "There's people from Newhaven here. I'm surprised. Those old girls dress up nice." He grinned. "Did I say thank you? I'll get on my knees if it will help. Thank you for accepting Britany's being here. Are you all right?"

She smiled as he leaned to kiss her. "You're welcome, Farm Boy. Now find us a seat before I have this baby right here on the floor with the band playing In the Mood." Across the room she saw Harriet speaking to Ruthie. "How does Ma look?" For a minute, Matt processed her words, then saw Harriet. "So now you call Harriet Ma?" She was walking toward them when the waltz began, "Stay here, Tinkerbell," he said, "and watch this." He met Harriet, placed her right arm on his shoulder and took her other hand in his. "Hi, Ma, Let's show these folks how it's done."

"I'm old and I'm not your Ma."

"No?" His laugh caused other dancers to glance their way. "I remember you dancing the waltz with Dr. Silverman. It looked like you two invented it. So come on, my mom didn't teach me dance for nothing." Grinning like the buffoon she was calling him, Matt danced her around the room and by the second round he could tell Harriet was enjoying herself. "I love you, Ma. Have I ever told you that?"

A mean Polka followed. "Not bad, Ma." Matt marveled at her grace. "Did Ruthie tell you Britany James is here?" He watched her expression change but she didn't miss a step. "Marigold and I decided we can handle it, can you?" Her eyes were throwing daggers, her lips in a firm line. "You could chew her up and spit her out without so much as a blink of an eye, Ma, because she hurt your daughter, but you know I will never hurt Marigold and I won't treat a childhood friend that's gone wrong badly, either. Will you give me that, Ma?"

The Polka ended and the Maestro called for the dancers to rest while Dan Gates stepped up to the microphone. "One of your own, folks. Dan Gates singing the song he composed for his wife the day he asked her to marry him. It is to an old tune we will recognize."

"Unbelievable, that's what I'll say…Darling you were what I longed for…take my hand…" Dan walked to the front row of people sitting at tables, and Ellen arose, "No one else have I ever longed for, take my hand…wear my ring…Unbelievable, we will always say….." Smiling Ellen joined in as they did a slow dance around the floor. The song ended and the crowd went wild, clapping and whistling as Dan and Ellen bowed. "Here's another old and familiar tune," Dan said, "join us." Laughing, everyone was singing and dancing to the songs that followed when at last Dan said, "Everybody, let's do the monkey…"

Suddenly the music stopped, those dancing slowed. Later, Andrew said it reminded him of a carnival ride coming to a stop, a carousel bobbing along until everyone could get off. But Daniel had seen Ruthie motioning across the room, her expression one of fear and taking that into consideration he was scanning the room, wondering what was happening. Suddenly the Day of Praise in the Park came to mind. Christ Church and Shining Light had combined to hold a special day during the summer at Newhaven. What had been an innocent day of two churches coming together to sing praise and witness was suddenly thrown into danger and chaos when Walden escaped the jailer and fired into the crowd. Miraculously no one was hurt but that was only by God's grace. "People could have been killed," was repeated again and again. Now, some inner warning was firing in his mind, get people to safety. Pray God's grace comes down.

"Pray." He said to Ellen. "Pray, Andrew," he said, reaching out to his friend. And the word went from one of the group to the other as they dropped to their knees and began to pray. People who were Christian saw them and joined in. Ruthie was clutching Britany's hand, while her friend with the strange name and pony tail watched the scene unfold. What he saw would stay with him all the days of his life.

"A man," he would tell for years to come, "A man dressed in a brown suit came through the door, he was tall, angular, confident. I knew that by the way he walked, he walked as if he owned the earth, his eyes were on Britany but he saw the people on their knees praying and his expression was one of disdain and contempt, his laughter began as a chuckle, gaining volume as he walked to stand in front of Britany and I will never forget what he said although I could not understand his meaning."

"You will not give to another man what is mine. I will bring pain into your life to make you regret. Woman, do not think to deceive me. I know the thoughts of your mind and desires of your heart. You cannot be as you have cast lot, I am strong because of who I serve and there are no prayers on this earth to break the chain of my master…for he has granted to me the keys to his chamber. You feel fear, it is nothing to compare to what lies in store for you. Throw aside this plan you have imagined, it will never come to pass. You will hear me in the air waves, see me in high places and feel me when the earth shakes. I will be there."

Ruthie holding Britany's hand felt her tremble and then the man with the pony tail was catching her in his arms. As Pookie glanced up the man in the brown suit left but the smell of sulphur was in the room and only he heard the words Ruthie uttered; words he would revisit in the days to come.

A lone clapping of hands began, joined by another until those on their knees heard the whistling and the clapping gained momentum. "Well done. Bravo." Praise rang out and then as though it had never stopped the music began.

"They think this was entertainment, part of the ball," Daniel said to Ellen and Andrew. "We must pull our wits together and allow their belief to exist; otherwise we will once more experience pandemonium, such as what Walden created the day of Praise in the Park."

"What happened?" Andrew's body was shaking. Daniel put his hand on Andrew's shoulder but it had no effect. "Man, my teeth are chattering," Andrew declared. "I can't control what's happening."

Ellen lay her hands on Andrew's. "Do you believe in the name of Jesus, Andrew Graves?"

"I do." The shaking stopped, his teeth quit chattering. He straightened his body and clothes.

"Andrew, I pray peace for you," Ellen said as Daniel motioned he must bid the guests goodnight.

From the podium he said, "Friends, it has been a wonderful Hutson's Ball. Thank you for your attendance and in giving to those less fortunate. Now, on the Orchestra's behalf, please find your partner and dance with a grateful heart and after that let us join together in the last song of the evening.

There were those participating in the last dance. Nate and Mabel had left the table but Suze found herself gazing at the stance of a gentleman in her direct line of view, he seemed familiar? Other than the people of the churches she knew very few who lived in the Cape. When he turned to scan the crowd she saw his face and stifled a gasp. What was he doing here? She stepped back into the shadows. He could not see her but she was certain it was him. She saw him clearly.

Chapter Eleven

"I could not believe the people thought it was all planned," Daniel's aunt confided as they were collecting the children's toys ready to go home. "When the orchestra swung into Old Aung Zion, there were smiles on the faces and happy tears as voices were raised in friendship until next year's Hutson Ball. I'm told, comments were overheard, "this was the best one, yet. The timing and staging of that fellow in the brown suit was amazing. It gave me chill bumps. I felt the war between good and evil. They really did it well. All that and no one knew it was not part of the event." A sobering expression on her face, "please, be careful going home and in the days to come. I could not take the heartache if I lost you."

So went the talk, and one could only reflect, as did Ellen and Dan, good and evil walk side by side, and only the people with changed hearts know the difference. Throughout eternity one's passion is to own the person and control the world while the other looks on with compassion, giving to each person the privilege of acceptance of keys to the kingdom, the devil may roam the earth but God owns the world.

"It is very troubling," Ellen said. "That it happened right in our midst and few are wise to the fact."

"How do you think Ruthie feels?" Daniel knew she was weary, as she tried to unclasp the pearls. Lifting her hair off her shoulders he was able to undo the small clasp, and the pearls fell into his hands. "There you are my love, your Grandmother's pearls that Ruthie will wear one day."

"She's grown, Dan, in wisdom and strength. I may have given birth to Ruthie but God gave her grace."

"It is our job to protect her as long as we can," he said, "and when she leaves us…" He became quiet.

"Yes, I know." Ellen sank onto the bed. "I had hoped this would be a memorable gathering but what happened puts a damper on how one feels. I don't know, Dan, we've been told to be watchful over Ruthie because there are those who would seek her out to wrongly use her gift, but how do we do that without smothering her and allowing her to have the privileges as other children her age?" Exhausted Ellen lay back as Dan removed his shoes and edged in beside her.

"How did we do this?" He ran a thumb across her hand. "We actually took two sets of twins dressed and fed to Hutson's Ball, helped with emceeing, entertaining and lived through an unexpected interruption and now we are home, kids in bed, reliving the night." He sighed, heavily. "I didn't think there were enough hours in the day to cover that much territory."

Ellen giggled, "And they were so out of it we put their jammies on with them sleeping." She turned into his arms. "What did Harriet's sitter do to wear them down?"

"I think it was all the people oohing and aahing over them." His arm went around her. "Have you ever slept in an evening gown before?" His voice was warm with sleep creeping in.

"No, have you ever slept in a tux?" She couldn't keep from yawning. "We could try it tonight. I believe we can do it." He didn't answer; already his breathing was even with a slight pearl now and then. But Ellen rose after a few minutes, her mind on something Ruthie said. "God told Andrew's friend he must decide who he would follow. I think the Holy Spirit is calling to him."

"He said you uttered a scripture, Ruthie. Do you remember the scripture?"

"I remember what the man said to Bethany. I think I can recall the scripture..."

Ellen had yawned along with Ruthie. "We'll talk tomorrow. All right Sweetums?" Now, she went to the sunroom and looked out on the garden Daniel had so meticulously built for her. In the moonlight the angel's wings seemed to hover, as though someone was there. Ellen stood still, watching and in the shadows she saw movement. A tall man stepped out of the shadow to stand staring at their home. Had she known, there were those who suffered the aftermath of the uninvited guest to the Ball. In the late hour, following, the man responsible for it all would visit and stand in the yard of her friends, making plans for revenge. Their lives were better than his. It did not matter he had opportunity to fulfill his dreams of life. He had chosen a different path, one that appeared lucrative but was deceiving bringing downfall and destruction. In his madness he stood next gazing on the home of Andrew Graves.

Andrew was gripping Anne's hand so hard she ask, "What is wrong? There's something you aren't telling me. Was Marigold upset you allowed Pookie and Britany to attend the ball?" She paused in speaking to study her husband. "I can imagine it was upsetting for her and Matt is defensive." She sighed. "It's because they almost lost her, Andrew. Is that what's wrong?"

"No." His voice sounded strange in his own ears. "It's the guy in the suit. I think it was Walden. Few people know in his college days he was in acting classes, some kind of drama team. He said he loved it and if he'd thought he could've made it, he would have pursued acting as a career."

"You never told me that before. Why?" She sat for a moment. They had put Andy to bed and changed into robes. They were sitting in the love seat at the end of their bed and for some reason Andrew had reached over to hold her hand. "I know something is bothering you. Just tell me, now."

"I'm a grown man, Anne. You know my short comings more than any person in this world. I've done about everything a man can do that's wrong but Harper and Dorothy Gipson saw something in me they said was worth saving. Walden's not the most important thing in my mind. But I remember how he loved the art of disguise and he became an expert at it." He rose up from the love seat, "Let's lay down, I want to see you while I'm talking to you. It's important." He pulled the sheet over their feet. "Something happened tonight that I don't understand. When the guy in the brown suit passed by me, and I'm sure it was Walden, he said, "your next, don't think you have escaped." It wasn't what he said so much as how he said it. I had a feeling I was listening to the devil. I looked around to see if anyone else heard him….and they were all paying attention to what Daniel was doing. Daniel was encouraging everyone to pray. How did he recognize something was wrong so quickly?"

"From the time I knew Ellen, she was different, Andrew, and then when she met Daniel he was too. I think the Lord brought them together for a reason, just like Harper and Dorothy had a bearing on your life."

"What about us? Is there something wrong with us?"

"What do you mean is something wrong with us?" Anne laughed. "We haven't been in this faith business as long as they have. They had a background that helps them understand what trusting

Jesus is all about. I was raised without anyone telling me there was a God. I did hear it at school…but I think that's the difference."

"Where I came from, folks knew. But tonight, Anne, I recognized the meanness in that guy, I know it was Walden in disguise. But Daniel recognized him in a different way, a way that said he was of the devils work, and Walden is, Anne. He threatened me as he walked by…what else will he do, he wants blood…mine or yours or Andy's to clean the slate where he thinks I wronged him."

"Things like this didn't use to bother you, Andrew. It was like water off a duck's back. Why now?"

"Because I'm different and I don't want him hurting you or our son."

"Then you are going to have to trust the Lord, Andrew. That's part of growing in grace. Trusting."

"Ellen taught you that, how to trust the Lord? You just do it, huh?"

"Yes, she did but I had to exercise it on my own."

Andrew began to laugh softly, as he pulled her close. "That's how you stood up to me, you trust in him that you could." He kissed the back of her neck. "No telling where I'd be now if you hadn't." He yawned."I think I can sleep now, but Walden, if that was him, scared the daylights out of me."

Newhaven

They arrived back in Newhaven. At Suze's house Nate started to get out. "You needn't get out, Nate. "No, no, I can make it to the door by myself. Goodnight and thank you for letting me ride with you."

Closing the door firmly, Suze shot the lock and sank against it, her back to the door. Breathe, she said, commanding her body to slow and accept the fact she had seen him. She was near tears. He had lied to her. He wasn't an engineer. But what was he? Her heart ached with his betrayal. He had accused her of not trusting him. Why should she? Tonight, her fears had come to rest. He was not who he said he was.

The ding of the computer continued, informing her he was trying to reach her. She undressed, hung up the beautiful dress Britany bought for her and went to bed but could not sleep until she unplugged the computer with its merciless ding that she knew in her heart was him wanting to explain. He had made a fool of her. A dry sorrowful sob welled up in her chest. She choked it back; she would not cry for him. Stephen Silvi was as lost to her as the day Wade died and she realized she would never see him again.

Two blocks down, Mabel said to Nate, "Suze seemed unusually quiet on the ride home, not two words."

"Tonight's Ball was full of energy. I imagine everyone's feeling it by now. I for one, need to head on down the road." His hand was on the door. "I did have a few minutes with Britany. I met her young man and I must say the pony tail is misleading. I thought he'd be one of those stuffed up persons full of himself but he comes across as an intelligent person."

"Meaning a pony tail is not what makes a man or breaks him." Mabel knew Nate was trying to make a decision whether to kiss her. It was something a woman just knew. A slight flush rose to her face, instead he said, "Correct. You look very beautiful tonight, Mabel. Now, tell me, what about us?"

Pastor Levi of Shining Light Church

Leah peeped into the study. Levi was on the phone. What she had to say would wait. She listened.

"So it was a good Hutson's Ball? You said the place was crowded."

"I thought you should know some of your people were there. Nothing goes on that's risky. But something happened. Several people think it was Walden and maybe it was, no one knows where he is. The thing is this; something unreal happened, you might say surreal. Dan said he felt like the devil was present and God laid this urge upon him that the people should pray else harm would come to them. I ask him how often that happened to him and he said not often, the last time was when Ruthie was kidnapped and he thought of the day of Praise in the Park, and he couldn't push it back."

"You believe him?" Levi liked Daniel Gates upon first meeting him. He was sincere in his faith,

"You met him. He led music for your revival. How did he come across?"

"I know," Levi agreed. "He seems solid as a rock." He was quiet a minute. "Yeah, I believe him, too."

"You know what I'm preaching on Sunday?" Joe planted a tease. "Yeah, and I might, too." Principalities. Right? We struggle not against flesh and blood but against principalities, against power, against the rulers of darkness of this world, scripture found in Ephesians, right?"

"You got it," Joe replied. "Let me know how it goes." The phone went silent.

"I heard that," Leah said, entering the study. "It sounds like something riveting happened at the Ball. Just think, we could have gone and experienced it first-hand." She smiled. "I'm teasing, if it's what it sounds like we get enough spiritual warfare right here on church ground."

Levi studied his wife; the pregnancy was changing her features as time was changing their bond of love. "By the grace of God we have a guideline on how to live through these tumultuous times. When we put on spiritual amour, it doesn't mean we won't suffer the pains of others intentions, it means God is with us as we go against the enemies of our soul."

"Or," she added, "as the enemy goes against our soul. I seem to understand that meaning better."

Chapter Twelve

At the Cape with Ruthie

The house was quiet the next morning when Ellen awoke. Daniel had emceed the program after a grueling week at work. Not only was he the boss but two of the men had a virus and were unable to come in to work which meant Daniel unloaded the big trucks after the shop and office closed. The night reserved for the Ball was one he promised he would come home early and he did. Right now, he was asleep.

Lost in thought, Ellen wondered what repercussions they would all face from the visitor to the ball and wondered that some folks, in fact the majority, thought the whole thing was staged, but it wasn't. Ruthie was standing by her side and must have spoken her name to bring her out of her reverie. "Morning, Sweetums."

"You didn't hear me call your name, did you?" Ruthie snuggled up to Ellen. "I like when we have time together."

Ellen gave her a squeeze. "Me too, you're my first borne and that's always special and you know what? That special grows through the years right on into adulthood. Then when I'm old, you will say I wish I wasn't the oldest and have to take care of Momma and Poppa."

Laughing, Ruthie said, "I won't either." A serious expression came upon her. "Momma, do you want to know what I heard last night?" Ellen nodded. "Momma, I think it is from the Bible. It sounds like the Bible but there's something different. He knew it though, on the last it was a message just for Britany, and Momma I don't think anyone else heard what I did, I am to tell you and you will tell the others because it is too hard for me."

"All right, tell me." Ellen tucked cover around both of them and prepared to listen to her daughter.

"He said, "I was deceived, overpowered and prevailed, ridiculed all day long, everyone mocks me. Whenever I speak, I cry out proclaiming violence and destruction, though the Lord's word is in my heart like a fire shut up in my bones and I am weary of holding it in, I hear people whispering, they wait for me to fall, saying then will we take revenge of him, but I remember the day when the Lord was with me and my heart was tender, now it is cold as stone. You will not leave me. You are mine. I plotted the course, nurtured you with forbidden nectar; you will not give to another man what is mine. I will bring pain into your life to make you regret you cannot be as you cast lot. I am strong because of who I serve. There are no prayers on earth to break the chains of my master. He has granted me the keys to his chamber. You feel fear, it is nothing compared to what lies in store for you. Throw aside this plan you have imagined. It will never come to pass. You will hear me in the wind. You will see me in high places and feel me when the earth shakes. I will be there."

Ruthie's eyes rolled back in her head, she did not rest but talked it through without stopping. Her skin appeared old wrinkled and cracking from dryness, her voice had become hoarse and Ellen was shaking her to come out of the reading. "Satan turn loose of my baby," Ellen commanded. "You will not have my child; she is sancti-fied, set aside, to the risen savior. Leave, you cannot have my child. By the blood Jesus shed on the cross, and rose again, I command you in His name to leave."

Daniel stood just inside the door. Rooted to the spot, he could hardly believe what he was seeing. He felt helpless, whereas earlier he had known to pray, coming from a deep sleep, he was sluggish wondering what had suddenly wakened him; he found his way this far but his feet would go no farther. Pray, his slow-moving mind now demanded. Pray. "Our Father, who art in heaven, hallowed be thy name, they kingdom come, they will be done on earth as it is in Heaven…"

Ruthie responded, "Give us this day our daily bread and forgive us our trespasses as we forgive those who trespass against us and lead us not in to temptation," Ellen joined in, "but deliver us from evil for thine is the kingdom and the power and the glory forever. Amen." Ruthie smiled. "I like when we all pray together."

Now Daniel moved into the room, griping his wife's hand as he put his arm around Ruthie, all the while willing Ellen to stand and shake off the tragedy that could have happened. The three held on to each other. "To God be the glory," Daniel whispered, listening as Ellen and Ruthie added, "Great things he hath done."

Ellen's hands were cold. She and Dan hugged with Ruthie between them.

It was only later, when Ruthie decided to make hot chocolate, Daniel asked quietly, "do you realize what just happened?"

"I was not aware, at first, listening to what she was telling me the man in the suit said, I was trying to place what he said, it sounded like scripture and I'm pretty certain it is either from Jeremiah or Ezekiel, where the Lord is talking to the prophet and is disappointed with the children of Israel." She stopped to take a deep breath, "I felt my child was being taken from me, and when I looked at her, right then in front of my eyes her skin was changing and I knew he had taken scripture and used it to his advantage and we cannot do that… and a phrase came to me, a most horrible thing has been done…and I know when we locate the scripture those words will follow and that will be a sign to us we have found the scripture. But I don't know the meaning of his words, why would he quote scripture?"

"If it is Walden, according to Andrew he is a master of many things, his IQ is way up there but there's a chance he has damaged his mind in using the very drugs he was giving Herm and Britany, because possibly he has been using them for years and while they sharpened his skills in some areas, impaired other." Daniel's own color was beginning to come back though he was never aware it changed, as he studied Ellen she was not as deathly white as when he first took her hand and as the skin tones were changing in her face her hand was not as cold. "We need to bring our friends together and ask Brother Joe and Levi to join us. I don't know if it is Walden or if his anger is directed toward Britany or just whoever steps in his way."

"What about Ruthie?"

"Let's observe and if she seems not to have suffered perhaps she should not be put through the discussion. Don't we want Ruthie to have her childhood as long as possible? Too soon, when her gift is found out, there will be those who infringe on her."

"I agree," Ellen replied. "I think I'm better now. For a while I felt I was wrestling with the devil."

Daniel pulled her close, kissing her forehead. "You were but God is with us."

"We will never forget this weekend; It could have ended in tragedy." Ellen felt physically weak. "Praise God it didn't." She sighed, "And we must act natural as you teach your class. It was then she remembered before going to bed she had glanced out the window of the sunroom to the garden. For a moment, she had thought there was a man standing in the shadow of the angel. "He was here, Daniel."

It was men's Sunday to take over at Christ Church. Daniel was teaching the second grade boy's class. Everything was going fine, scripture had been read, the penny offering taken for missions. "Do you have any questions before we dismiss?"

"Mr. Dan," a little freckled face boy asked, "Where does the devil live. Can he see us?"

"I know," his buddy answered. "He lives in people's backyards and he watches us."

"But God's stronger, right Mr. Dan? And He watches over us doesn't he?"

Worship hour was upon them. With Christ Church pews filled, additional chairs were set up along the back wall. The singing was exceptional, everyone seemed ready to put the summer days behind and embrace fall. Voices rose in song of praise and thanksgiving.

In the second pew Daniel waited impatiently. In view of all that was happening he couldn't help but wonder if the Lord had laid a sermon on the pastor's heart that would either shed light on the event or lead the members to examine their own lives further. The little boy's question had opened a door Dan could not shut. Ellen sensed Daniel's anxious spirit, reached over to lay a hand on his arm. In a few seconds the nervous energy dissipated.

"The reading of scripture," Pastor Joe said, "is found in Titus, chapter two, eleven through fifteen. "Please stand as we read together. "For the grace of God that brings salvation has appeared to all men. It teaches us to say, "No," to ungodliness and worldly passions, and to live self-controlled, upright and godly lives in this present age, while we wait for the blessed hope, the glorious appearing of our great God and Savior, Jesus Christ, who gave himself for us to redeem us from all wickedness and to purify for himself a people that are his very own, eager to do what is good. These, then, are the things you should teach. Encourage and rebuke with all authority. Do not let anyone despise you."

"Please be seated." For a time, standing silent, Pastor Joe studied his people. "Do you remember the words of scripture to Isaiah 60:1?" Two hands were raised. "Can you quote it?" Arise, shine, for they light is come," a voice from the back recited. "This scripture is telling the people to stand strong, troublesome times are upon them. Paul knew they would be tempted to hide out, and even absent themselves from those Jesus worshipers. How could they ignore so great a love that Jesus laid down his life for them? When all they had to do was live a certain way? Let's think about today."

"What does he expect of us? Because he died for us, and we ask him to come into our lives scripture tells us He expects we speak truthfully, not to let our anger cause us to do wrong, nor steal that which belongs to another, we must not engage in unwholesome talk, or do any of the things mentioned that goes against living a life worthy of our calling. We must be gentle and kind, patient and loving as we allow peace to live amongst us. That is saying no to the things we are not suppose to do as we gain godly wisdom."

"Now what about people who have no concern for others and do those things anyway, who anger, hurt and mistreat those around them. Are they godly people? Who do they belong to?"

Daniel recognized the voice the minute it sounded. "They belong to the devil and he lives in our backyard, don't he Mr. Daniel? We studied that in our class today." Daniel shrunk a little in his seat.

"And Tommy," Pastor Joe stepped beside the boy. "If someone shows up that makes you think any of those thoughts, will you run to the nearest adult and tell them?" Tommy was nodding yes. "Church how should we handle those who would cause problems?"

"You said encourage them if they're good and rebuke them if they're bad." Tommy wore a frown. "Pastor Joe, how do we rebuke the bad spirits?"

"Thanks for helping me with this sermon, Tommy." Pastor Joe returned to the pulpit, "Should you encounter a bad spirit, remember they often are hard to recognize and harder to work with." He scanned the congregation. "Does this happen? Yes, scripture tells us there will be false prophets, wolves in sheep's clothing, people who have no love for God or fellow man, evil do-ers. How do we handle that? First, we must be soaked in the word of God, but there will be times we must command that bad spirit to come out, in Jesus name by the blood he shed on the cross and by his victory…rising from the grave. Remember we do not wrestle with flesh and blood but with the darkness of the world."

As the service ended Daniel listened to the comments people made as they shook Pastor Joe's hand. "A bit severe, weren't you?" You don't really think something like that could happen do you? It is all to scary to think about. And last, "I believe you, Pastor. Thank you." Daniel's mind was speeding ahead to the days to come and the terrible scene in his own home that morning. He checked with Ellen; it was time for the group of believers, to come together, that evening at their home. They sent out a text.

* * * * * * * *

They arrived, the friends who had developed closeness over the years; they were believers who recognized Ruthie's gift. "I think Ruthie is young to have to realize the magnitude of the gift," Dan said, "Though Ellen explains as Ruthie grows older. She accepts her gift cannot be used in vain, for someone who wants only to see the works and not the healing powers given."

"She is young," Brother Joe said, "What happened as you described it, to her this morning, was an attack, no doubt to test how strong she is at this point in life. As she matures she will be quick to know He is there and will lead her through each situation. Right now

Ruthie is of pure heart and sweet nature, she feels people's pain and in compassion reaches out, it is her touch brings calm where there's chaos."

"I was asked if Ruthie is physic," Pastor Levi said. "And I first of all was new to this and secondly wondered how the person knew about Ruthie's gift, are there those outside this group informed?"

"Unfortunately yes," Dan replied, "Because at the moment, Ruthie's intention is to help someone in need."

"Haley's not here," Dorothy Harper added, "But you remember she was unsettled when she returned from prison and Ruthie led her to the Lord, out in Ellen's garden. She said Ruthie explained that God loved her and she could have peace and calm in her troubled soul but she felt Ruthie's gift was quite evident in how her life turned around. Again it was a matter of listening, praying and laying on hands."

"So what do we need to do to keep Ruthie safe?" Andrew's eyes were dark with concern. "We all love that little girl. We may not understand how what she does happens but we've all experienced the gift through Ruthie's compassion. She may be one in a million, but she is our little friend, we need to be aware something could happen to take her out of our midst. What are you thinking that it's Walden?"

"I have a question from our pastors," Matt and Marigold had come in after discussion began. "From this morning's sermon, Pastor Joe, do you think it is possible Walden could be demon possessed, an evil spirit could have claimed him?" Marigold's eyes were pinned on the reverend. "And where does discernment come from that we will know a demon is trying to get into our world?"

"When you were saved, Marigold," Brother Joe explained, "The Holy Spirit moved into your heart. It is the work of the Holy Spirit to watch over you, lead you in paths of righteousness and do unction for you when you are troubled or someone is trying to overcome you. You will know."

"My experience," Andrew added, "at the ball, showed me there's more than one thing at play in Walden. He felt confident and his opinion was nothing could hurt him, because we know in a set of different circumstances he could have been shot, at least apprehended, but he walked in and walked out, safe. Yes, he may be on some mind altering drug, but he looks at you crazed and bold, with eyes that says you can't touch me." Andrew shuddered. "I worked for the man and I'm telling you sometimes I thought he had made a pact with the devil."

"I can't answer that about Walden," Pastor Joe replied, "But he does not appear to be following the Lord, does he? Then who has he allowed to become his master?"

"According to what Ruthie told Ellen, he said the master he served was more powerful than any other." Dan looked to Ellen to justify his words. "He said I am strong because of who I serve, no earthly person can break the chains… Maybe I'm not saying it word for word, but you get the meaning?"

"Then what is our recourse?" Matt's time was short on leaving. "I'm sorry, I have to drive back to the farm in time to do a few tasks in preparation for tomorrow's work and I want to know my part in this."

"Pray, Matt." Pastor Joe was grappling, searching for words to impress upon the group, "This seems like something happened in Jesus time, but this very thing may become more prevalent with the ways of our world, presently. Society condones less and less the acts acceptable today that once were not even considered and when our world becomes corrupt leaving behind God's commandments and Jesus teachings, then yes, these things happen, we have seen a preview in Walden. What must we do? We must pray, our only defense for Ruthie is to be watchful but in the meantime talk to the Lord."

"Then, we are as Matt," Pastor Levi offered, "our time is short, there's work to be done in preparation for tomorrow, all the tomorrows, we are to watch and pray. God gave Ruthie a gift to use to his honor."

Matt and Marigold left shortly thereafter, as the group continued discussion and left an hour later. What was said in their midst would not be spoken beyond the day, but the plan to pray continually and watch carefully was set in motion, as Pastor Joe said, "To last a lifetime. Ruthie's life time."

* * * * * * *

"It seems a bad dream,"Marigold said, as Matt kissed her goodbye. "Our being apart seems a bad dream," he replied. "When this harvest is finished, I'm coming home."

Chapter Thirteen

Newhaven's Shining Light Church

From the window, Suze saw the Pastor and Leah drive into the church parking lot. It was time for Sunday night services. Those services were few in attendance, but more personal in sharing and studying the word under Pastor's direction. Though she was reluctant and would never bare her soul.

"Have you ever felt troubled, to the point you didn't know what God wanted you to do?"

Without a moment's hesitation, Suze found herself thinking about the situation of Hutson's ball. He was supposed to be in another state and yet, he was there, in the Cape. A trickle of apprehension coursed her veins. Was he dangerous? Was there even an ounce of trust left in her for him?

Oh, how she wanted to speak out, confide in someone, but they would brand her an indecent lady and she was not. Some small reminder went off in the back door of her brain, there where she kept hidden her relationship with him. They were friends, nothing more, but were they? Why would he lie to her?

She found her mind skipping to the hall beyond the Sanctuary, nearly finished and she supposed her room, next. They pursued the renovation relentlessly but thus far no one had opened a can to paint. Her eyes held on pastor's wife. From what she heard, the pregnancy was coming along satisfactorily. Suze couldn't help but look. No longer was she sitting comfortable, instead her legs were stretched in front, while the Pastor seemed not to notice as he was busy explaining scripture. Then something he said took root and Suze forgot her pastor's wife's discomfort.

"Recently I was asked to sit in and listen, when a brother was caught up in something that clearly was not of God but more into the works of the devil. As your pastor, it was horrid. It was nothing to be blamed on church family. This was one man's choice. I understand he is a wealthy man but right now he is running from the law and yet he can slip in and out of places to do his damage."

Suze sit straighter, interested in Pastor Levi's story, her interest peaked thinking his story connected to the Hutson Ball where something definitely took place but was kept quiet. Her heart felt the pain that followed; she would not say his name but she wondered since he was there, was Stephen Silvi a part of that?

"It seems when a person throws in with the devil, they appear to have certain powers. As Christian's you can understand this, the devil slips in and out of life, and this man has an uncanny nack for slipping through barriers and showing up to spout scripture he has twisted to suit his need for the moment. It's scary. But we have God's word to counter that person. Through scripture we have been warned."

"Pastor, are you saying a person taking on the devils help might even take on his characteristics?"

"Exactly." Levi paused, thinking. "Our world is changing; the wiles of the devil are very much present. Could someone please read first Peter, five and verse eight."

Suze found the verse in her Bible, "First Peter five, and verse eight. Be sober, be vigilant, your adversary the devil walketh about as a roaring lamb, seeking whom he may devour." Later leaving the church she couldn't help thinking Pastor Levi was preparing Shining Light Church for a fight with the devil.

* * * * * * * *

Walden laughed, the pitch of his laughter rising beyond the high ceiling. He had his spies everywhere. They dressed as the congregation, not wanting to arouse suspicion they were any different, though they were there to gain ground. He was building his following, as the pastor said, his congregation. His Hutson's ball people were already gone before he arrived that night. He had to go it alone. He could barely stand against those Jesus-talkers.

Dressing as a police man, he examined his reflection in the mirror. "Pretty good, fella, you're a handsome man, oughta make the women's heads turn today." His laugh burst into the room, resounding the walls, coming finally to a slow ebb... "Of course you gotta take care of that little Ruthie girl, maybe take her to another state and leave her." Pointing to the mirror, he said, "We gotta get rid of those Jesus worshipers, you and me. Then we can never forget dear old sweet Andrew."

"You are not my master," he said suddenly. The voices had sounded in his head. "Where have you been?" Walden sneered. "Don't you know the answer to your own question? I've been going to and fro on the earth, and from walking up and down on it."

"I am a self-made man. Of course I sprang from my momma's wealth. She doted on me, sent me to the best schools. You know I'm educated more than any of these country bumpkins and you know I told you let me prosper and I don't care if there's ever a good deed done in this world by anyone else as long as I get to the top. My physical prowess has gained momentum. One day I'll fly and that will be better than sliding unnoticed into the places I have to go." The man in the mirror smirked. Walden smashed his fist into the reflection and the man disappeared. "Let that be your warning," he cried. "I am the one."

At The Cape

"El," Anne's voice sounded troubled, over the phone, as she glanced at the hour on the clock.

"What's wrong?"

"Could I come see you on my way to work?"

Five minutes later Anne rang the doorbell and Ellen pulled her into the room, hugging her friend. "I heard problems in your voice. Sit there," she said, "so I can sit opposite and look into your face."

Anne gave a pitiful laugh. "All I said was your name."

"I know you that well, all those times through Nursing Class. Look at us now; You, on your way to work."

"And you have two sets of twins, so you are staying home, let's switch." Then Anne looked down, her hands folded in her lap. "El, what the man in the suit said to Andrew was upsetting for him and now me." A tear dropped onto her wrist.

"Anne," Ellen said gently, "I know you too well. Yes, you are worried over Walden but I sense there's more." It was then Anne sobbed. Ellen rose up to find the tissue box and sit down to wait.

"You know Andrew and I want another child." She raised tear filled eyes to Ellen. "The doctor told me Friday, due to the accident I won't be able to conceive. There's no hope, but I haven't told Andrew." An unexpected sob shook her chest. "He'll be so disappointed."

"Listen to me," Ellen took her hand. "You have a lovely little family and much to be thankful for."

"But Andrew thinks another child will bless our family more than anything else can."

"Your love for the Lord and each other brings blessing, Anne. Yes, babies make us happy and tie us together but if a baby is the answer to a marriage why are there so many divorces?"

"I'm afraid, Ellen." She allowed Ellen to put her fingers under her chin and raise her head until they were looking each other in the eye. Ellen's expression ask the question. "We have been through so much, Ellen. What if it tears us apart?"

"I don't understand, Anne. You have Andy, your sweet boy, replica of his daddy. If there's no other way, isn't he enough?" For a second memory flashed through Ellen's mind. "Anne, Andrew felt responsible for you having the bad accident. He said he demanded you bring Andy home when the roads were in bad condition. Have you discussed this with him, at all?" Anne shook her head.

"When Andy was nearly killed by the hit and run driver, Andrew began to change. Harper said he found Andrew lying prostrate on the bathroom floor praying for Andy to live. Anne, talk to Andrew I don't think he will be angry over your not being able to conceive, he will remember all the times he hurt you. I'm sorry to bring it up but that's why I think Andrew will rejoice he has you and let the other go."

"I hate to disappoint him, Ellen."

Ellen reached across to pull Anne into her arms. "You've always been that way. You are not responsible for other people's happiness, Anne. You work for a doctor, for heaven's sakes, he tells you those things; you cannot make other people happy. They have to work on that project themselves."

Anne rose up, "I have to go to work, Ellen." She sighed, "Thank you for trying to help me."

She was already to the door with her hand on the knob when Ellen said, "He's not the same Andrew, Anne. I believe he's changed and loves you and Andy above everything else. Trust God. Trust Andrew."

* * * * * * *

Anne didn't know whether to laugh or cry, Laugh with gladness that Ellen saw the change in Andrew; that he loved her, or cry because she still felt so unsettled inside. She had accepted being told she could not bear a child due to the severity of the accident. For Andrew she had seen the special doctor her own recommended.

The warning light came on and she turned quickly to put gas in the car. She was digging in her purse for her credit card when she recognized the little red car cruising past, a blonde haired lady in the driver's seat. Anne wondered what were the chances of two women needing gas in their car at the same place every week. By the time the lady found an available pump, they were in next aisle to each other. As the little girl waved and blew kisses, Anne realized she had seen the little girl many times at this very location and the little girl always smiled. It was her smile made Anne's heart ache; if they had a little girl, somehow she just knew their baby girl would look like the one throwing kisses.

Keeping her back to Anne, the mother never showed her face. Anne had not lost sleep over the fact the woman was unfriendly. Truth was, with Andy staying with Harriet and the mystery surrounding Britany there was enough talk as to why Britany was marrying Pookie. Anne had plenty other things to think on. Add to that, she felt if they couldn't have a baby, she and Andrew had their own worries; she needed to keep to herself. Now all she could think was she should never have talked to Ellen.

"Hi," the little one was hanging out the window, her hair little damp ringlets around her face, her hands reaching to Anne.

"Oh, Sweetheart, you might fall out. Please scoot back into your car seat." The little girl did as Anne asked, the smile not leaving her face. "Ma'am?" Anne tried to get the mother's attention, but the woman ignored her and Anne knew she had seen her. Resigned, Anne got in her car and drove away.

Chapter Fourteen

Britany's run in with the authorities meant she had to drive into the Cape to face the consequences. Now she stood before the judge and he was speaking.

"I would have thought better of you, young lady."

The Judge was talking to her. Britany was stunned. "Sir, are you speaking to me?"

"I believe I was, Miss James." Judge Roy Crump squint his eyes and then reached for his glasses top of his head. "You don't remember me; I was your daddy's best friend's son. I used to visit the farm with my daddy." He waited for recognition in her eyes. "Crump. Roy Crump."

Her eyes lit up. "Little Roy?" She stepped closer. "Why you grew up, didn't you?"

"I'm the youngest on the circuit, sitting in for the old codger, today." He leaned down and whispered, "I shouldn't have said that, don't tell him." He grinned, as he glanced around the courtroom.

"Why are you last, and why here, couldn't you just pay your fine and go home?"

"No, sir, I back talked. In fact I stomped my foot when they told me how much, just for jiggling across the white line on the highway, and that got me something to do with treating the Police officer bad and then my mouth…so they said,"contempt of court.""

"That's ridiculous. Who did that?" Roy Crump was climbing out of his judicial box, removing his robe and coming down to talk face to face.

"Some woman, named Edna Sparks."

Roy Crump began to laugh. "She's at it again. I declare, she's trying to find me a wife. Are you married?"

"About to be, if I can pay this fine."

"Forget it I'll mark it off the books." He leaned against the lawyer table. "So you are getting married. To whom, do we owe the honor?"

"George Edward Fernandez."

"Who?"

Britany blushed. "I believe it's actually Edward George Fernandez." When he shook his head, she said,"Pookie?"

"Pookie?" He stood straight, peering into her face. "The Pookie who works for Andrew Graves?" She nodded. "You can do better than that."

"No, I can't. Pookie, it is." She sat down in the chair. "Do you marry people?"

"Of course, by the powers vested in me." He grinned."Want me to perform the ceremony for you two? Shall I wear a suit or the robe?"

"Wear the robe. Let's impress people." She found a piece of paper in her purse."Here's the address, the time and I'll pay you that day."

"No charge Britany. I had so much fun on your daddy's farm I should be paying you."

"Be there, then," she said. "If you have any friends, bring them, I'm kind of short on such."

He read the information. "Next Friday?"

"No, this Friday, can you make it?"

The best made plans often fail. A hurricane battering islands Southwest of Florida brought foul weather to the area, but the worst centered on Applegate Farm, destroying the beauty carved out by Britany's workers. In a flash of lightening, wind and rain, the yard was obliterated with debris, half the roof was gone on the front of the house and it was less than one week until Britany's wedding.

The Cape's phone lines were busy. Marigold received three calls.

The first was from Anne.

"Are you going to the wedding?" Anne asked. "Me? I have no choice, they asked Andrew to be Pookie's best man; well actually he did. Why are you still home?"

"I wasn't feeling my best this morning and Harriet said she would fill in at the Shoppe."

"Do take care of yourself. It's really close to your date, isn't it? Someone asked me who is Britany's bridesmaid? I don't know. She stayed with Mrs. Hisaw from Newhaven after she was released."

"They will be in our group, eventually, by way of Andrew, won't they?"

"There's always the worry that Walden will show up. Andrew said his voice that night at the ball scared him to death. He doesn't want to run into him again but he seems to consider Britany his possession. I have to get to work. Marigold, call me if you need anything. We want a safe delivery this time."

The second call was from Ellen. "Dan and I just got a call from Britany. I was surprised. She wants us to sing at her wedding. It's in our church." Ellen listened to the sad quality of Marigold's voice. "I know. It seems she doesn't really feel welcome in Newhaven church since the park incident and Herm's not been released, yet. What do you want us to do, Marigold? Our friendship is important. We treasure you."

"Honestly," Marigold replied, "She may not be as much a threat married as she is single. She has chosen Pookie for some reason. I don't know him very well, but he seems a nice person. Maybe some of it will rub off on her." Sensing the silence on the other phone, Marigold apologized. "I'm not feeling quite so ready to embrace her, if you know what I mean. When she no longer chases Matt, we'll see."

"I feel bad about the whole thing."

"Knowing you, Ellen, you are devising a plan where you can witness and ask her if she has accepted the Lord."

"Isn't that what we are supposed to do?" Ellen asked softly. "God spoke to my heart, Ellen but I feel I have to be aware if she changed or is the same. Only time will tell and if there's enough time, in our group we will learn whether she has a desire to know our group without creating a disturbance over our men." She realized Ellen was quiet, "I have a child on the way and M.J., Ellen. This woman has blatantly and publicly tried to mess with my marriage. I owe it to my children to be on guard, but I would never mistreat Britany as she intended to mistreat me."

"You mentioned change, Marigold. People think they have to change before they give their heart to the Lord but it's the other way, when they accept him, they begin to change because he is helping them."

"As in all things, Ellen, people have to want to change, otherwise they never do."

"I hope you and Matt attend the wedding, Marigold, because down the road I have this feeling Britany will be sorry for her actions and need your forgiveness."

"Matt and Britany started school together. I can't imagine Matt not attending, Ellen."

"Then Britany must see you standing by his side, my friend."

Not sure why she wasn't feeling well, Marigold returned to the bedroom. M.J. was sound asleep. The early morning rising for Marigold to open the shop took its toll on her son. She closed the bedroom door and pressed the upper lock into place. In case she went into sound sleep and M.J. woke up she had to know he couldn't get out of the room without her assistance.

She must have drifted off. The ringing of the phone awakened M.J. It was Harriet, checking on them. "I'm all right, Ma. How are you?" She gave a small chuckle,"so they told you. Yes, first Anne and then Ellen called. They are attending. What should we do, Ma?"

"It is a difficult decision," Harriet replied. "Even I feel the temptation not to go. When someone messes with your child it puts you on the defensive and you really want to beg off."

"But Ellen feels that down the road, Britany will feel remorse and ask for forgiveness."

"Some people never feel remorse," Harriet replied. "It takes moving a mountain." She took a deep breath as she finished her thought. "Sweet Heart, you and I have been blessed to find each other, it may be the Lord expects us to put our petty differences aside and honor his word. I can do that, can you?"

"You know, Ma, with you and Matt on each side of me, I believe I can make it." Trying to push bad memories away made by Britany's own hand, Marigold shook her head. "I don't know why things affect you more when you're pregnant. You didn't have anyone to go through it with you, did you, Ma?"

"No, but I do now."

* * * * * * *

Wedding Bliss

Not wishing to appear too impetuous the group arrived to take seats as friends to the bride. Pookie, on the other hand had his family. The church was beautifully decorated with huge bouquets that filled tall urns, elegant arches with satin ribbons led from the aisle to the place where the bride and groom would stand beneath a taller arch entwined with lily of the valley and baby's breath. There, the Judge would hear their vows. Ruthie was taking it all in as she watched for Marigold.

"It's breath taking," Anne whispered to Ellen. "Britany has spared nothing. I passed through the concourse and the décor there is the same. When this girl throws a wedding she means business."

Ellen gave her the look only friends understand. "Let's hope." They shared a smile.

Marigold sandwiched between Matt and Harriet remembered her own wedding, arranged completely by Matt with love and devotion and the smile that played around her lips was noticed by Matt. He tipped his head and kissed her lips. "I bet I know what you are thinking, Tinkerbell."

"No," she whispered, "you don't."

"That little mountain chapel. You wore a gown of lace; they played The Rose, because I ask them to."

"Right on, Farm Boy. How did you know?" Her eyes were dewy and his were too.

"Because I was thinking no one could beat that." He reached for her hand and kissed the palm of it.

Pookie and Andrew walked to the front and stepped in place as the first chords of the organ swelled and burst into the Wedding song. Judge Roy Crump followed them, turned to face the people and ask that all rise as the music flowed and Suze started her trip up the aisle.

"That woman is from Shining Light Church. I met her in the back," Anne whispered to Ellen. "I wondered who would be her attendant." Suze proceeded down the aisle as Britany entered the double doors to the auditorium. "Oh, my goodness." Anne was blown away. "She looks absolutely beautiful."

Ellen smiled, remembering Anne, the shy quiet girl she had befriended during their days of training. And now she was nervous and talking, completely unlike Anne, sweet, beautiful wife of Andrew Graves. "Andrew and Pookie don't look so bad, either," Ellen whispered into her ear. "Your dream boat."

Nothing but the best, Marigold was thinking. I just hope it sticks. We never heard a word about Britany and Pookie dating and now here they stand in front of Judge Crump, decked out in the finest money will buy. Thank you, heavenly Father for this little reprieve you are giving Matt and me. Faintly she heard the words, you may be seated and noticed Ellen and Dan were standing to one side of the piano ready to sing while Pastor Joe's sister accompanied them. Ruthie was watching her. They waved discreetly.

"Dearly Beloved we are gathered here to join this man and this woman in Holy matrimony." Matt was squeezing her hand. "If anyone here knows just cause these two should not be joined together, let them speak now or forever hold their peace." The room was as quiet as a coffin left in the rain. From that point on, the room breathed on an even keel, the attenders' were mere mortals partaking in a ceremony that customarily was built on trust laced with everlasting love.

It was when the Judge said "by the power invested in me by…" A loud boom sounded in the street. The stained glass windows shook and rattled as the carpet runner in the center of the aisle buckled and raised off the floor. Though shocked, Andrew and Pookie remained at the front with Britany, Suze and the Judge, but to a man those attending rushed outside.

In the street a tall man walked a distance, turned to face them and began to speak, "You will not give to another, what is mine. I will bring pain into your life to make you regret. Do not think to deceive me. I know the thoughts of your mind and desires of your heart. You cannot be as you have cast lot; I am strong because of whom I serve. There are no prayers on this earth to break the chain of my master for he has given me power and the key to his chamber."

The air was filled with the smell of Sulphur but there was no fire, no wind to cause the drift. Those who attended Hutson's Ball whispered, "It is the same man. Why is he here? What does this mean?"

"A magician's trick," someone whispered. "He has no power." At that moment, a huge limb fell from top of the oldest oak and landed within two feet of the man who whispered. "That could have killed me," he cried out. It was then they heard the laughter, beginning a low rumble, picking up pace, to become demonic, a sound that could curdle the blood of the innocent.

"By the power invested in me by the state of Missouri I pronounce you husband and wife."

"Whatsoever God hath joined together," Britany and Pookie joined the Judge, "Let no man put asunder."

"Matt?" Marigold had felt immediate relief when he returned to stand by her side. But his teeth were clenched and his chin set at that stubborn angle she knew so well. "Matt, I don't think we can stay for the reception." His expression was misleading. "I'm sorry; you can stay if you want to."

"Babe, I don't want to stay without you. What's wrong?" By this time Harriet was leaning in to hear.

"I think my water just broke." Matt and Harriet glanced to the cushioned seat of the pew. A small spot appeared fresh and the proof was the puddle in the floor directly below the cushion. "Please," her voice was begging. "When everyone leaves for the reception down the hall, then help me. Please, let's don't make a scene. This is Britany's wedding. Let her remember it without incident."

"As if that can happen after the loud boom," Harriet replied. "That probably affected you."

"Please, Ma, I'm very uncomfortable and now we have to buy a new cushion we may not be able to match." Marigold was near tears. "It's not the cushion, Ma, I think I'm in labor, I've got to go."

"I'll call Hattie to stay over with M.J., I'm going with you."

* * * * * * *

Suze overheard their conversation as she was searching for the ladies' room. The couple seemed familiar. It was then she saw a man who reminded her of him, his hair, and the way he was standing. He wore proper clothes for a wedding but she couldn't remember seeing him inside. She was being silly. He was a thousand miles away, and then he turned.

She covered the surprised gasp, seeing Stephen Silvi, as large as life again. Why was he here? She hid behind a folding screen. Barely out of sight when he turned and walked past her, she nearly fell to her knees. He was carrying some kind of device; all she could think of was a two way radio. Why? Her heart was thumping crazily in her chest and she was so nervous she thought she'd fall face first.

"There you are," Mabel laid a hand on Suze arm. "They are ready to take a picture of you in the wedding party. Wasn't Britany pretty in her wedding dress? It is one of the prettiest I've ever seen." Suze felt like a lamb being led to slaughter, going down the hall, listening to Mabel make small talk in animated sentences about Britany's wedding. "You looked pretty, too, Suze. Imagine her asking you to be her bridesmaid. Now when she throws the bouquet, you be sure to catch it."

The hall was long with many doors; Suze feared he would pop out of one at any minute. "Mabel, when the photos are finished, if there are any of our people going back to Newhaven, I need to go home."

"This is probably the best thing we will have all year long and you're going home?"

"My stomach is tied in knots." Suze glanced away when Mabel gave her that questioning look.

"I don't know anyone going that way, but let me tell you the latest." Mabel's face glowed with happiness.

It was a day of happenings, good and bad; Bad that the authorities considered the men's explanation of the boom that rattled the windows and rolled up the carpet runner in center aisle, a threat. Suze's experience was unsettling and Mabel wore a glow of happiness and on her left hand a diamond.

"We were driving home the other day," Mabel explained, "when Nate said, have you walked in the park lately?" Of course I said no. Until now it was still hot and we have so much going on, when I arrive home I just want to relax. Well, it was a loaded question."

"That park was the first place we kissed and I asked you to marry me." He said. You were only thirteen, I replied. "Well, it should count," says he. "So let's go check out the new walking path." Whatever for? "The park is the perfect place, well lighted, people always present and there's only one inlet and they built a rise or an incline for those who like a little challenge." You think of everything, I said. But was I surprised. Once we got there, Nate sank down on his knee and was very gallant. I thought he was reacting his teenage days, but he wasn't. I'll never forget what he said."

"This is where our courtship began, Mabel. Since that time we've lost each other, found each other and now I want to make it permanent. Mabel, will you marry me?" Nate fumbled in his jacket pocket and said, "I'd like for you to wear this ring." Mabel smiled holding up her hand. "I'm so happy, Suze."

Suze had to wait and ride home with Nate and Mabel. She loved her friend but tonight she wanted to wallow in her own grief. Even now she heard the computer ding, meaning an email arrived. I won't answer, she whispered. Anger coursed through her followed by hurt and tears. She hadn't realized she had fallen hard for Stephen Silvi. When they first began talking and she ask his name he had said Regenald, but he cleared that up later as his internet name. Their courtship hadn't even begun and now it was over. She had been communicating with a man that had filled her head with lies.

Hours later she hung up the dress Britany had bought, at the time not knowing any reason why Suze would need a dress. Suze became distrustful, rumors had circulated that Britany was trying to break up the Langley boy's marriage to the girl who decorated the church and now, Suze saw them when she was hiding and they were leaving because his wife was in much pain. Suze's own pain bordered on anger.

She hit the doors top panel; hit it again, again and again. She was weak. Weak in despair, Suze sank onto the bed. She'd never done that without removing the spread. She left her shoes on. It was in the night when she awakened, her feet swollen inside the shoes; the spread was dirty and Suze felt the tears running down her cheeks. She hadn't known she cared for Stephen Silvi or whoever he was, she had just thought she was lonely and enjoyed the conversation they shared. If she felt such pain what had Matt Langley's wife felt if Britany had tried to destroy their marriage? For some reason she felt the need to pray for Matt Langley and his wife and she better pray for Britany and her new husband, too. All she could do was wonder where the Langley's were going with his wife in such pain. The way he was helping her and the look on the girl's mother's face couldn't be good. Now Suze felt ashamed that she had wasted tears on Stephen

Silvi, but her heart still hurt. She must pray to ease her heart and she'
pray for the couple, too. Finished praying Suze found herself by the
computer. *There was a message. I send love on Angel wings.* Why would
he bother her with those words when he hadn't felt it necessary to
keep her trust.

Chapter Fifteen

"Seeing you in pain hurts me," Matt said, "Are you calling the doctor or the hospital?

Marigold closed her cell. "My doctor is out of town? They have called her but she may not arrive in time…" Marigold dissolved in tears. For some reason everything seemed at odds and it shouldn't.

"It's all right, Babe. I'm here." He pulled into the hospital parking lot. "And we're here."

"I'm glad, Matt, but my doctor stressed over and over she wanted to be the one deliver our baby."

"You've carried it all by yourself, Marigold. I'm here. I'll do what I can." He was helping her now.

"I feel so emotional. I think it was going to the wedding. I should have listened to my inner being. I shouldn't have gone." Matt had a firm grip on his wife and a small suitcase in the other hand.

"Then why did you, dear?" Harriet glanced at the paraphernalia they were carrying in.

"I'm so tired, Mom. It's been hard doing everything and then the wedding was stressful."

"You shouldn't have gone. Why did you?" By now they had Marigold in the bed.

"For Matt, Mom, for Matt. She was his childhood friend. But I didn't know I was going into labor."

In the shadowed corner of the room, Matt started to rise, instead his jaw flexed. Why would they blame him? But she was right. He had left his own family to help his dad. He'd left a pregnant wife.

The labor went on through the night, Marigold's hair was damp. Perspiration stood in tiny little beads on her lip. Harriet placed a damp cloth on her forehead. "Do you want me to go home, Matt?"

"No, Ma, its good you're here. I heard her call you Mom, does that happen often?"

Harriet's chuckle was half sob. "No. I noticed but I didn't say anything, afraid she'd stop."

"I'm worried Ma, it's taking too long, what happened last time surely won't happen again, will it?" Matt rubbed a hand over his eyes. "When she miscarried, she didn't want anyone to know except family. She didn't want to be reminded of our loss or people feeling sorry for us. Thank God we had M.J."

Harriet leaned over Marigold, her hand lightly on her forehead. "She's sleeping, Matt. Those pills relaxed her. She's been restless; let's straighten the sheets one more time."

They were interrupted when the doctor and nurse came in to check Marigold. When finished, they studied the chart a few minutes and then turned to speak to Harriet and Matt.

"Mr. Langley?" Dr. Nelson extended her right hand. "I believe we better do a C-section. Your wife is very tired. If you plan to join us you need to get washed up, put on a sterile gown, shoes, hat, gloves, the works and in about an hour we will have a baby." She smiled at Harriet and shook her hand. "Please, relax." She smiled. "Someone will come for you and keep you close by. They are working on the room. It will be cleared and ready to go by the time Mr. Langley is dressed."

* * * * * * *

Anne heard the news from Hattie and called Ellen. "They left Britany's wedding to go to the hospital."

"I had no idea this was going on. I thought maybe Marigold was tired from sitting. What can we do to help?" Ellen glanced at the wall clock. It was past two and Dan just came in from a meeting. "I don't think they want help, just to have this baby without complications, she's been in labor a long time."

"We need to be praying." Ellen's voice ebbed away. Her daughter stood before her, fully dressed as though going somewhere. "Anne, Ruthie's trying to tell me something, I've got to go."

* * * * * * *

Ellen had seen that expression of sadness on Ruthie's face before. "What's wrong?"

"Momma, Marigold is in the hospital. There's a problem. I need to go to her."

"Let me get dressed and tell Dad we are leaving."

The hospital corridor was quiet except for the whisper of the nurse's shoes as they traveled the halls. Ellen and Ruthie found Harriet in third floor's waiting room. A pillow, blanket and a bottle of water had been brought in. Surprised, Harriet rose to greet them with a welcoming hug.

"What are you doing here?" Tired as she was, Harriet smiled. "We heard and came to sit with you. As bonded as Ruthie and Marigold are, how could we not?"

"I'm glad for your company."

"How are things going?"

"They are getting ready to take the baby."

"C-Section?"

Harriet nodded. "They had Matt to gown up so he can be with her."

"Is the baby all right?"

"As far as we know. I haven't seen anyone since they called Matt. Surely he is still with her."

The three watched the hands on the clock move around. "I wish I could see Marigold," Ruthie said.

"It's not allowed, sweetie. You can check on Marigold after the baby is born." Ellen noticed tears running down Ruthie's cheeks. "Sweetum, what's wrong?"

"I don't know, Momma. I feel sad and when I look, I see the baby wrapped in a little striped blanket and there's tears on Marigold's cheeks.

"Is Matt with her, Ruthie?" Ellen remembered M.J.'s birth. Marigold had hidden her pregnancy, fearing the displeasure of Matt's mother, but Matt's mother never intended to come around. Unless Britany James was his wife, she would pretend there were no grandchildren, while she waited. Marigold had been strong standing up to the woman's rejection, but she had developed a fluid problem which left untreated could have lost either her or the baby's life. "I pray she is strong enough to deliver this baby and then perhaps she can forget the turmoil she's been through. Surely he's there." Ellen was picking up certain feelings, too, and it made her uneasy. She glanced quickly to Ruthie.

"He's there," Ruthie nodded.

"Harriet, did the doctor imply there were complications?"

"No. but the way the doctor and nurse looked at each other bothered me." Harriet shrugged. "Sometimes you sense things and then question every move thereafter."

"Did they decide on a name?" When Ellen asked Ruthie spoke up. "They have two they are considering, Maggie Sweet or Margaret Jane. The J is Harriet's middle initial and Sweet was her childhood name." Ruthie sighed. "We need a little baby girl, we have plenty of boys with Andy and the twins." Ruthie noticed they weren't talking, because they were worried.

"I didn't know she knew my maiden name." Harriet chuckled, "I didn't know they were considering my middle name." She winked. "I guess Harriet was a bit too much to tack onto a new born, wasn't it?" She rolled the name across her lips, "Margaret Jane." Yawning, she teased Ruthie, "You always have the inside scoop with Marigold, don't you?" Harriet was immensely pleased they would use her name, she couldn't stop smiling.

"I think they will call her Margaret because it was her mother's name." As if answering to her name, they heard a baby's pitiful cry trying to gain strength, hanging in the air and then a warble of silence.

The tiredness left Harriet's face, replaced by a smile at the same time tears welled up in her eyes. "I think our baby has arrived. She was a strange little song bird, wasn't she, Ruthie? I guess Ellen will have to give her lessons." Ruthie's smile in return was brilliant as Ellen placed a kiss on Ruthie's head.

"Now we can rest," Harriet said, great relief shining through her words. "I can't wait to see this little girl." Hearing the door to the room open, she turned as Matt picked her up and swung her around.

"We got our little girl, Ma, Pink as a pig's snout and crying up a storm. Did you hear her?" He was beaming as he hugged Ruthie and then Ellen. "I was sweatin' bullets. Marigold havin' babies is hard on me." He waved at Harriet as she collected her purse and hurried in.

Harriet embraced Marigold. "Oh, my child, you have done good. Praise God from whom all blessings flow."

"Were there problems?" Ellen's expression was serious, as she entered and waited for an answer.

"We don't think there are, but the doctor says they have to run tests. I don't know why."

Marigold was propped against the pillows holding a little dark haired baby wrapped in a striped blanket. "What did you name her?" Ruthie's eyes met Marigold's as she whispered. "I hope I love her as much as I do you."

"You will, Ruthie. You will. We are going to make you special to her. This is Margaret Jane but we are going to call her Maggie. What do you think?"

"I like it."

"Climb up here by me. I think you need to hold our little Maggie."

Ellen saw the streaks on Marigold's cheeks and she remembered Harriet saying the doctor and nurse shared a strange look she felt had to do either with Marigold or Maggie. Now she studied baby Maggie. In Ruthie's arms, content and sleeping away the child appeared completely healthy. But there was a mystery, she felt it. In a glance she saw, even now, tears were quietly dropping from Marigold's cheeks onto her arms. Then, Ruthie turned, handed baby Margaret Jane to her mother and as Marigold wrapped her arms around the baby, so Ruthie wrapped her arms around mother and child. Ellen joined them. Scripture came into her mind and as it arrived she saw a baby, born helpless, barely breathing, the doctor was massaging the baby when the baby gave a feeble cry; the mother accepted her child and began to rock back and forth, back and forth. The sound of women crying came to their ears, how long, how long were they praying, their hearts and minds as one. Ellen was aware of Matt on one side of Marigold, holding her, his face a ripple of sadness as Marigold cried. The time evolved, words of praise countered the sound of women crying until Ruthie sat to one side, smiling, as one would, complete in the joy of the Lord. Then she said, "We can go home now."

* * * * * * * *

Anne tried the hospital. Then she tried Marigold's phone. Matt answered. "Tell me," she said.

"A baby girl, seven pounds three ounces, dark hair, pink skin and beautiful."

"The Mom or the baby?" Anne teased. "So, can you stay with Marigold and not have to go farm?"

"Do me a favor," Matt asked. "Look out the window and see if it appears we will get rain. I may have to return to the farm, unless the men stored the equipment and shut everything down."

"Oh, Matt, it's a full moon and beautiful. The air feels like rain, but I don't know."

"Good enough." It was then; Matt heard Anne scream. "Anne, what's wrong?"

"He's here, Matt. The man we saw when Hattie hit him on the head with the skillet. Why would he be looking at Harriet's house? Andrew's working late. I can't go home, besides M.J. and Andy are already in bed but why would he be outside Harriet's home?"

"Call Andrew, Anne. Andrew says Walden's crazy either from the drugs he's used for years or he's sold his soul to the devil and he plans to stalk every person who he feels wronged him."

"But I haven't, Matt, I barely know the man, only his reputation."

"Andrew knows him, Anne. Years ago Walden decided it was Andrew found the money he had hidden in an old car; money he stole from the drug lords down in Mexico. We've been through this before."

"You mean that's why he had Andrew thrown in jail. But Walden was in prison, Matt."

"Anne, don't ever trust him. Trust what your husband told you. The man is out for blood. Walden is."

"Matt. He's coming toward the house, but there's a car pulling in the drive."

"I'd say get a gun, Anne except the boys are there, too risky. Go hide, Anne I'll call the police."

Turning in her drive Harriet recognized him. It was Walden. She aimed the car toward the front of the house, her lights sweeping around caught him full force. He began to run. Harriet gunned the motor and went after him. She saw him drop something or was he throwing it away? Walden jumped the hedge, crept along in the shadow, on his knees lest he rise up and she run him down. Harriet knew the arbor over the back entry was barely wide enough for the car, but she went for it; who did he think he was dealing with? She was no teenage girl, nor was she reluctant to leave tire marks on her million dollar lawn, the lawn she had babied until she didn't know what else to do. Driving along the fence banked by roses, she saw a few clawed spots and laughed, he was that shaken, then she heard the train on the tracks and thought she saw a tall figure hiding near one of the side cars. He would return. Walden wasn't one to let anyone get the best of him. Turning around she back tracked, looking and seeing nothing to finally pull into the garage and was out of the car and into the house without a hitch. Tonight was as good a night as one could wish for to be rid of items stored in the back closet, she knew exactly where her husband's golf clubs were, she laid a couple out turned the lights off and backed up to the counter ready to show him what a lucky person he was. You are out of your league, she whispered.

The hair at the back of her neck stood on end when the lights went on. She grabbed an iron and was ready to swing. Anne's eyes were big as saucers. "Harriet, this has been a terrible night and just now some crazy person was driving all over your front lawn. I think all the work and babying you have done has been destroyed. I'm sure there are tire marks all over it and didn't the irrigation system run this morning?"

"This afternoon, late," Harriet replied glumly. "I'll call someone and have them make repairs."

"You better tell them to bring rolls of sod," Anne replied. "It's bad. But that's not all, Walden was here. I couldn't reach Andrew's phone. There's a blind spot in that area. That's ridiculous for a law office."

"What would you have done, Anne, if Walden broke in?"

"Just in case, I put the boys to bed in your big closet since there's air and they thought it was fun. Like camping out, and I found Hattie's skillet," tears came into Anne's eyes. "But I was scared so I got in the closet with the boys and locked it tight. Why in the world would you have a closet like that in your bedroom, Harriet?"

"For times just like tonight, Anne; you did right." Harriet was picking up the phone. "Now let me make a call and then I'll tell you about the baby and how Marigold is doing, then we'll put the boys in a real bed." She was dialing, and then speaking. "Yes, it's me. I'm afraid my lawn was uprooted tonight. Could you oversee repairing it tomorrow? I'd like it to look as though nothing happened by tomorrow night."

"There, that's settled." Harriet rubbed her hands together, a strange gleam in her eye. "Anne, you never know what you are capable of until put to the test."

"I'm sorry about your lawn. I thought he'd left and came out to check, that's when I saw the car."

"Rule number one, Anne, always keep yourself and the boys safe, nothing else matters. Things can be replaced, not our boys or yourself."

* * * * * * * *

Daniel received the news from Matt. "So while we were meeting trying to figure out how to capture Walden or at least keep him from harming our families, he was out scourging them as we spoke." He shook his head wearily. "Thanks, Matt. I hope your family keeps progressing towards good health."

Andrew glanced up, expectantly, "we've put in a day, coming after Britany's wedding."Good news?"

"Not really. Check your phone. Matt said Anne was trying to reach you. The signal is low on mine but he was able to reach me and if it's working perhaps we should call our wives." He glanced at the newcomer to their group, not knowing if he was reading the man right, or not. "You said you studied Walden's record. What did we miss? I feel there are more important things you're not telling us."

"You've covered it very well. But I must warn you. You can't operate outside the law. If Walden's after your families, that warrants your concern but not only state but Federal are now interested in him. He doesn't have a license to be a doctor, or for that matter write drug prescriptions. That's only a small portion of his wrong doing. As far as we know, he hasn't killed anyone yet but now his foolish and reckless behavior makes him more dangerous than before. He will become a public nuisance again because that draws attention and he loves to be in the lime light."

"How long have you been on the case?"

"Long enough to follow him to every state in the Union, what he does is a far reaching business."

"But," Harper was relentless when he wanted information. "How do you meld yourself into lives that make you appear acceptable to society, to me, even."

"We use any or every means available, such as Internet but what Walden's capable of this time has us on a short leash." A tight smile crossed his face. "But that can backfire on you, on a personal level."

"What do you mean?"

"My wife has been gone many years, so it's acceptable if I should meet someone. What actually happened I was to find and build communication with someone to this area as we found Walden was born here, attended school and seems to still have business dealings. I was to tap into one of those sites for lonely people to find someone that might give information and it happened a woman in Newhaven took the bait. She was such a nice lady, I enjoyed our conversations but she became suspicious of me and now she won't pick up her phone and certainly not correspond as we were doing in the beginning. She really mistrusts me."

Harper sensed the man's disappointment. "You sound as though you care for this woman."

"There's the problem. It is highly unprofessional to become personally involved. To be authentic, in trying to convince her I was a lonely man looking only for conversation, I forgot the rule."

Harper studied the man that had contacted Dan and told him they were in over their head; the Feds were tracking Walden due to his association with the drug cartel. "I believe you've fallen for her, just listening to you. Fate pulls us in, doesn't it? But we never know what's around the corner."

Chapter Sixteen

Britany

The wedding reception was over. Britany's people were cleaning up, bagging trash, removing white table cloths and asking what to do with the decorations. "You take them," she said, "If you want them." All the chairs were folded and stowed away, the tables carried to another room, and the flowers picked up by a local nursing home in hopes they would cheer up the residents. "What now?" She asked Pookie.

"Your plans were to stay at Applegate, but the storm took care of that." Pookie was watching her expression to see if she agreed to the plans he had made. "I thought you might be tired. I reserved a room at the new place out on the highway. They have just opened. Are you all right with that?"

"I am tired," she replied. "Thank you for taking care of it." She yawned. "Yes, that's wonderful."

By the time they reached the five story motel, Britany was asleep. Pookie opened the door, gathered her, wedding dress and all, into his arms and carried her into the motel, across the lobby and down the hall to the room. She didn't stir as he removed the dress, tucked the sheet around her and left to go back down for their luggage. "You are very kind George Edward Fernandez," she murmured. "That's a nice name. It has a ring to it." George smiled. She had no idea what she was saying but he wondered if she remembered, her last name was now Fernandez. Britany James Fernandez had a nice ring to it.

It wasn't the way he imagined spending his wedding night, watching late movies, but he had married Britany with good intentions. He would take good care of her and she would never wonder why he made contract with her concerning being married for life, possibly to a woman who would never love him. There were worse things; he had lived through worse many times. He was a patient man, it was his love and devotion would open the way for them to enjoy the days of their lives together. It was her words that rang in his ears. When he asked why she chose him, she replied, "If I can't have Matt Langley for my husband, then it doesn't matter whoever comes along."

He considered the ceremony. There were enough people present. The reception was demanding, by the constant line of people wanting to wish them well, or was it curiosity? One day he would no longer be the understudy at Graves Law Firm. His name was on the door right along with Andrew's, but he knew his place. The reception buzzed, their first dance was the high light of the night.

Britany was light in his arms. She was a beautiful bride in a dress he imagined cost more than six months' pay he earned at the law firm. They were congratulated, applauded and hugged with people saying they were a handsome couple. It wasn't the first time he accepted the fact he was in love with Britany. If she never loved him and turned him away, his heart would not change. *Truly the words Til death do us part, took on new meaning.*

Four o'clock in the morning, George Edward Fernandez fell into bed and slept sound as a baby. The name was his, legal with no exceptions. He preferred to be called Edward.

His mind, too fuzzy to think a good thought; he ended up thinking at least the man who claimed he owned Britany hadn't shown up, unless he was responsible for the loud boom. Edward's body shook.

* * * * * * * *

The morning brought Anne home from Harriet's to find Andrew sitting at the kitchen table.

"I have a confession to make," Andrew admitted. "I wasn't working on a client's case after the wedding. I was doing work that we hope will coerce Walden into coming forward."

"That will never happen. Didn't Dan tell you he was at Harriet's house? It was scary. You need to be with us nights, Andrew. If you are helping Pookie, you are going to have to let him fend for himself."

"He's married to Britany now," Andrew stared out the window where daylight was breaking. "He is probably in danger, too. We had a stranger in our group last night that revealed Walden had been giving Britany mind altering drugs. There was a time she slept eighteen hours a day and the remaining six was too groggy to even know she exist."

"Everyone knows that, Andrew."

"They don't know for a time, she was made ward of the court, with her friend Nate and Mabel Hisaw guardians. Those two had no idea what danger they put themselves in helping Britany. He's crazy, Anne."

"You have said that all along." She leaned tiredly on the back of a chair. "So, someone is sitting a trap hoping to catch Walden, the man who eludes everyone and everything. Do you think he has supernatural powers?"

"I don't know if God allows that or not, I do know he pleads alliance to the devil. Does the devil allow a man special privileges? It scares me enough that I want no part in that."

"And yet, you spent last night discussing this with a group of men resigned to stop him." She yawned. "Andy's with Hattie, I need a shower and I have to go to work." She pecked a kiss on Andrew's brow. "Please, come home on time. We need you. Let someone else chase the crazy man."

"Someone else's family and friends doesn't seem to be under attack, Anne. Ours is."

Anne stood beneath the shower head letting the water flow over her tired body. How much more could they all take, considering the circumstances? Marigold's baby had arrived and they were all on alert, any member of the family could be taken. Walden's threat had not been dismissed. Andrew was asleep in his chair when she let herself out and headed for the office. The day was without incident; by late afternoon she pulled in to the gas mart, anxious to return home, when the red car entered the lane. The little blonde haired girl waved but the mother turned her back to Anne.

Neither woman would know how it happened; as Anne finished hanging up the hose she saw a flash of blonde hair; the little girl was out, in the line of traffic, the back door to her mother's car open. Anne shot between a pick-up truck and a motor home, grabbed her and clasp her to her chest. Scared, the little one was hanging on her fingers digging into Anne's shoulders, her cry alerting her mother.

For a moment they stood staring at each other. The mother was trying to comfort her sobbing child while her mind tried to adjust to facing the one she had wronged knowing she had aged, she who had celebrated every new convenience or luxury a woman could experience was now sick and haggard.

"Do you recognize me?" She held her hands out for her baby. "Come on, precious, come to Momma."

"I do. You are Clayton Walden's daughter, Summer, isn't it?" There was no warmth *in* Anne's voice. "Have you planned this or is it coincidental we fill our cars with gas every week at the same place?"

"Sometimes it's planned."

"Why? What do you want of me?"

"Could we park our cars and go inside to sit at a table and talk?"

"It's usually too busy and loud for conversation."

"Then meet me down the street at Lucy's Diner."

"I'm reluctant, but curious why you are stalking me."

"I am not stalking you. I have something to ask you."

"All right. Lucy's Diner." Without another word, Anne climbed into her car, drove the two blocks, went in and sit at the nearest table. Glancing around the room, she saw a wheelchair by the door, and was reading the sign above when the woman arrived. "You have a question for me" She asked as the woman sat across from her.

"Look at my daughter." Anne studied the little girl. "No, really look, who does she resemble? Not me."

Puzzled, Anne searched for understanding. What was it she said the first time she encountered the two? Memory whispered if you had a little girl, she would look just like this one, Andrew's resemblance. Suddenly her heart lurched. Could this be? Quickly she arose, picked up her purse and was leaving.

"Don't you want to know Andrew's daughter?" Quietly spoken but the impact on Anne could have been a bullet to the heart.

"How do I know this is true?"

"Try DNA, if you prefer or else listen to the circumstances. Your husband did not know then nor does he know now. I was pregnant when we parted company and you married him again." Anne was accessing her, she understood. "I know, I am not as pretty, as well dressed, nothing about me is the same."

"You are needing money?"

There was an angry flash to her eyes. "Are you capable of listening?" The anger seemed to tire her. "I have watched you for months; Trailed you, I know where you work, your friends, your salary."

"How would you know that?" Anne's eyes narrowed. "I'm at a loss; I don't know people who do that."

"Yes, you do." She leaned across the table and spoke quietly. "I am dying of Cancer." She leaned back, waiting for Anne to absorb her words. "I have no one to take my child." Sadness crept into her words claiming her expression completely. "You are a good woman and she is Andrew's child."

This is a dream, Anne was thinking. I will blink my eyes and wake up. But the two were still there, the little one sitting beside her mother, smiling at Anne in the most trusting way. "How old is she?"

"Does that matter? You do not believe me?" Snappy words hit Anne, bam, bam, bam. "Can you not see the resemblance? She looks nothing like me." Then it dawned on her. "Oh, you mean, have I been with Andrew....no, I haven't I was pregnant nine months, of course and now she is nearing her second birthday."

"When?" Anne was counting the length of time she and Andrew had been together. Almost three years. The dates worked and the child looked exactly like Andrew's baby picture. "What do you want from me?"

"November twelfth, is her birthday." For a moment her body shook, she grimaced. "I didn't take my pain pill." It happened again. "Would you excuse me, I must go to the car and get my medicine." Stooping she said to her child, "Sit with the nice lady and Momma will be right back."

What if she didn't come back? Anne pinched herself. "I am in shock," she whispered. Someone wants to give us a baby. She wants to give us her little girl. I can't believe this. "What's your name," she asked, not knowing if the child understood.

"Adeline. I two years old." Holding up two fingers she slipped off the bench and came around to Anne. "I have a boo-boo." They were admiring her boo-boo's when the mother returned with a photo album.

"This is her future should she end up in a children's home."

"Why would she end up in a children's home?"

"For breathing out loud, lady, if you do not take her, she will be shoved from one home to the next."

"Don't you have anyone? Family? Friends?" Anne sighed as the woman shook her head negatively. "If you have no friends, I can ask Andrew, I mean." She found her own thoughts scattered presently.

"Do you ever make a decision for yourself?" Tears were in Summer's eyes. "I see how you live. You know good people. You work for a doctor. You attend church. The truth is you are the one will see to her needs. You will love her. He may not."

Anne felt she was spinning away. "I take it you have this all thought out." Fresh beads of sweat broke on her forehead and upper lip. She took off the light scarf she was wearing. She wasn't good at decisions. But Ellen said she was different from the girl who had been beat down...

"They are getting ready to put me on Hospice. I know. I'm not certain I agree but it's inevitable." She cuddled her daughter close, kissed the tip of her nose and said, "I love you babykins. You are the light of my life. God has blessed me so much the last two years. Just having you made a difference."

"You don't want her seeing the procedures or what it does to you." Anne said softly.

"Exactly." The tears were running freely down her face now. She was grieving. "But I do want to know who has my daughter and I need to have this settled." Her eyes were luminous, pleading.

"How do I explain this to Andrew?"

"That one is on you. I'll be honest, I don't know. But if you could do a DNA test, you will know for sure my baby was by your husband, Andrew Graves." A pain hit her stomach again, nearly doubling her over as a great sob ripped from her and she set Adeline down gripping her own body.

"Didn't you just take a pain pill?" Adeline was walking around the table keeping an eye on her mother.

"I did." Summer Walden grimaced, "they work less and less.

That's why I need you to say yes."

Anne's mind was in a quandary, her heart touched with compassion to help the woman in her pain. "When did you have in mind?" Now Adeline was petting her mother, studying the tears on her cheek.

"Now." Summer's voice was weak. She slumped down into a chair for the moment laying her head on the table. "I've sneaked out of the house. I don't have long." she raised her head their eyes meeting. "I'm sorry I caused such problems between you and Andrew, but honestly he was with other women, too." Tears rolled down her cheeks. "Please, take my baby and love her. She's little and innocent."

"I have no supplies, no clothes for a little girl." Anne sought one last way out. "I'm sorry."

"In the car," Summer gasp. "I have everything. We have been on the block an hour waiting…."

Blowing out a big puff of air, Anne shook her head. "How could you do this when you are so sick?"

"I have no choice. There's no one else. There are papers giving you legal rights. Her papers."

"What's Adeline's last name, in case I am stopped?" Anne wondered that she could voice the question.

"Adeline Grace Graves." Trying to rise from the chair, Summer gasp with additional pain. "I apologize but I knew things might go easier if she had her father's name on the birth certificate. You'll have to take the car seat, or they might stop you. Grab that wheel chair by the door, please…"

Holding firmly to the wheel chair, Marigold waited for Summer to be seated and take Adeline on her lap. It was bulky as she tried to push the chair toward the door, it was practically refusing to move.

"The brakes are on, to keep the chair from rolling," Summer instructed, her voice barely a whisper.

"I know. I'm a nurse, I can't believe this," Anne muttered. "Have I lost my mind?" Summer was feeling the pain, her cries began suppressed, to break through in a strangled moan that soon reached pitch.

"Oh, dear God. Thank you, Anne." A sob caught in her throat. "I have prayed and prayed for this." Another great sob broke. "Please let me know how she's doing, my baby."

Anne pressed the chairs brakes, opened the car to remove the car seat. It had been a while since she worked with a car seat, nothing was going right. Finally she opted to put Adeline Grace in a seat belt until she installed the seat in her car. "This is crazy." The pressure was killing her. "Andrew will never go for this."

"He has too." Summer cried and her voice upset Adeline. Anne couldn't get the strap through the seat, the crying was turning into wailing and her own nerves were shot. It was then she felt someone's presence. A young man in uniform stood behind her; she was uncertain what branch he served.

"Miss. If you will move away I believe I can help you." He was taking over. Soon he had the seat in Anne's car, Adeline buckled in and noticed Summer was on the passenger side of the car. "Which one of you will be driving?" His glance came to Anne. All the stress had exhausted her, she felt desperate.

"Are you busy for the next hour?" Anne asked, wiping sweat with a rag she found in Adeline's bag.

"No, ma'am. I just arrived back in the states and got nowhere to go. May I help you?"

"Do you have a driver license and would you be in trouble if you help us?"

"No, ma'am, I don't believe so. Do you want me to drive this car?" He glanced quickly to Summer bent double, tears dripping off her chin and then back to Anne, sweating and frustrated.

"That's what we want. Now, Summer give this nice young man your address and I'll follow." To the soldier she said, "When we get there, we have to change those packages in the back seat to my car."

"Yes, ma'am. If you want I could stay with the lady whose sick." Anne stared hard at him and then Summer. "What do you say, Summer?"

"I'd like that." Her voice was nothing but a whisper, "until the others come."

"All right, let's move the packages, the diaper bag and that box to my car and we will go home."

"Kiss the baby for me," Summer pleaded. "Tell her I love her." Her sadness filled the air.

Anne felt like beating her head on the sidewalk. "This is awful. Horrible, Summer. Do you want to call this whole thing off?" Now, of all times she realized his branch of service. "Thank you, Soldier".

He nodded. "I'm glad to be of service, ma'am. Does the lady want to change her mind, ma'am?"

"No, please. Go, Anne, Summer replied. My number is in the diaper bag. Please take Adeline and go."

Anne watched as he helped Summer into the car; then they were out the drive and disappeared into traffic. In her own car, Adeline gave her a sweet smile and waved from the back seat as Anne's phone dinged. It was a message from Andrew. *I'll be late. Don't wait dinner.*

Anne called Hattie, but Harriet answered. "Oh, Harriet, I'm late picking up Andy. I'm so sorry. I'll explain it to you when I see you."

"Anne, the boys played hard all day. Outside of course, but Hattie has bathed and fed them and they are already sound asleep.

Why don't you leave Andy? He will be company for M.J."

"Thank you, Harriet. I appreciate your kindness so much. I've had a rattled day." Harriet laughed.

Arriving home, she pulled into the garage, let the door down and carried a sleeping Adeline inside. Laying her on the sofa and covering her with an afghan, Anne walked through the house. In Andy's room, little boy toys told the story. Then there was the third bedroom with a bed, dresser and chest of drawers. She pushed the bed to one side, then turned it a different angle and found more room available if she relocated the other two pieces. That done, she went to storage in the garage and found the crib Andy had used. A break-away-model, it didn't resemble a baby crib once she adjusted the height and the rails. She had left the mattress in the guest room closet and soon the two were assembled.

Using the only set of white sheets from Andy's cache, she remembered the lace edged set she had kept that someone had given her before Andy was born; a pillow in a frilly little case with a matching quilt. The pink embroidered roses edging both had not suit Andrew's taste for his boy at the time. Carrying Adeline in, she placed her on the pillow, removed the little shoes and socks Adeline was wearing and placed the quilt over her. With a big sigh, Adeline curled up and put her thumb in her mouth. For Anne that was new. She smiled for the first time since pumping gas that evening.

The whole ordeal had been traumatic. If it was for her, then what about Summer? Sitting on the edge of the bed she sent a message to the number she found in the bag along with the legal papers. "Summer, your sweet baby is asleep in my son's crib on a rose edged pillow and matching quilt. I'll send you a picture. I will take good care of her. I hope you can get well. Quickly she snapped the picture and sent it. If pain was any indication of severity, Summer Walden was very ill, as she said with her cancer.

Maybe she had learned something from Ellen, after all. This was no time to be vindictive over Andrew's past affairs that had broken not only her heart but her spirit, too. Adeline needed someone tonight and she had been chosen, evidently, otherwise someone else would have answered the call. She didn't know how they would handle the situation but Andrew was a lawyer, he would know. She was tired, she slipped out of her clothes, ran through the shower, and found a clean pair of pajamas. Surely he would be home soon. She would lay back and rest a few minutes before she found a sandwich to tide her over.

If Anne had known Walden was standing in the street making plans for his greatest adventure ever; she would not have been able to sleep. It was good she had closed the garage door leaving no one sight when she carried little Adeline into the house. He had kidnapped his own cousin and Britany, but this time his plan was to bring together all who had caused him problems. Britany because she married another man, far inferior to himself, Andrew Graves because he believed Andrew knew where the money he had stolen from the Cartel was hidden, and Suze who disdained his cousin Herm, he knew because while impersonating Herm she had refused his company and then there was little Ruthie, said to have a gift of discernment from God. He laughed. He had discernment but it wasn't from God. The one he served was much quicker to act. Of course he could be imaging he was able to do supernatural things because he chose to serve evil rather than good. Didn't every person make that decision? Only he had climbed the ladder to success while others failed. When he orchestrated an event, it always went off with a bang, take Britany's wedding. His laughter began with a chuckle and built to a diabolical sound that brought people to their windows, looking out, seeing nothing. He was invisible and someday he would fly.

The doctor had questioned that statement. "Mr. Walgreen, no one I know can humanely fly. Where did you get that piece of information?" Having changed his name in order to see the doctor, Walden had stared so coldly at the doctor; the man backed up into an adjoining room and locked the door. "You may go," he said from the other side of the door and laughing his insane laugh Walden left. He did not stop at the desk to inquire of his bill; he walked out because he knew he was invisible. His last doctor had said he had been hitting the drugs too much, naming the one he preferred most. That doctor disappeared. The Newspaper carried a sentence or two weekly about the poor man. Walden laughed. He had the energy of a twelve year old, mentality of the gods and the strength of a sumo wrestler. Life was good; Now, to contact his helpers. When those on his list started disappearing, he wanted them all at once in his chosen lair; therefore he must enlist the help of his people. Some people would do anything for a price and he had money. All they needed was a new born baby. There was room.

* * * * * * *

Daniel and Andrew pushed back from the table where they had been working. Four others had left.

"What do you think about Silvi's plan?" Daniel hunched his shoulders front to back. "We sit too long."

"I hear you," Andrew replied. "I didn't know how to take him at first, but I did a bit of checking. He is legitimate. We couldn't take the word of just anyone. My contact at the Federal office said it is true Walden is wanted in a number of states because he is the Kingpin behind moving contraband from another country to this one and then into the states. We probably have no idea the locations but Silvi does. They said we could trust Silvi but to keep his identity quiet because there are more problems."

"He's different. Ruthie told me by her mother's invitation, Silvi and Mrs. Suze Norman visited our garden and he isn't died in the wool believer but he is a questioning candidate." Daniel laughed, "Those aren't necessarily her words." Still stretching his body, Daniel added, "He did like the garden, though and Ruthie felt he liked Mrs. Norman."

"Our little Ruthie." Andrew raised questioning eyes to Daniel. "Do you worry? I mean, someone like Walden that's crazy and fabricates the most outlandish tales, such as Silvi says he has been on drugs so long parts of his brains affected and he has this grand delusion he can fly. Silvi said no doubt when he's high on the drug he does think he is flying. You know some think bugs are crawling on their face when there are none, so why not flying? Sometimes I have this feeling there's something Silvi is not telling us. Like if it's on a higher level, even than drugs. He's so polished, not just drug force, maybe Federal. Now, tell me, what about Ruthie?"

"I don't know, Andrew, but if you meant to say are we concerned over Ruthie's safety, yes and no. First we have to put her in the Lord's hands. He gave her the gift, we have to believe he will take care of her, but people like Walden are conniving and we wonder how evil is their evil? we can't chance it. Every child deserves the best protection their parent can give; it's just that we aren't with them every minute."

"I'm learning." Andrew took a deep breath. "Man, it's time to go home. Anyway, since Andy's accident I've seen life differently. I appreciate Anne more and can't imagine losing either one of them. I tell you when Harper prayed with me on that dirty bathroom floor, God's grace and glory came down and it stuck. I'm a believer." He picked up his brief case, "I just hope none of my old sins ever catch up with me." They stepped outside, glancing up at the moonlight; the town's new water tower was visible in the distance. "Do they work night and day?" Andrew shook his head. "Man, right now I'm glad I'm a lawyer."

Daniel laughed. "Yeah, I think they've set the date for filling it and that means dead line for the workers. You see how well-lit it is, I imagine there's two shifts. God's blessing on them to no accidents."

Chapter Seventeen

Andrew pulled into the second garage space. The house was dark, meaning Anne had a long day and was asleep. He checked Andy's room. Anne knew his habit. She'd left a note, *Andy's at Harriets.* He showered, set the alarm and crawled in bed. "You tired?" He spooned his body around hers. "Your new shampoo smells good." She always replied but not tonight it must have been a stressful day. He had to smile holding her in his arms. He had wasted several years running with the wrong crowd, after they were married, when he was associated with Walden. Once he had thought to beat Walden at his own game. Anne divorced him and he didn't blame her. He had treated her badly in his quest to out-shine Walden. If he had succeeded he'd be dead by now. Sometimes he thought Walden sold his soul to the devil. The man had no scruples. About the lowliest thing he knew Walden had done, wasn't the drug, or the way he used his wife's inheritance to buy his way up the ladder, he'd slept with his step daughter and messed her up for good. He hadn't thought of Summer in ages, why was he thinking of her now?

Summer had been fire and ice. Money was available; her momma was heir to a lucrative business. She had every luxury a woman could imagine but she was wild, said her step dad was to blame. He hadn't known what she meant for a long time, until her momma kicked her out. Anne was sweet and gentle. Ellen had taken her under wing and restored in her the confidence he had destroyed. Through the word of God, Anne learned she didn't have to bow and scrape to satisfy him, he was on the wrong track. Thank God for Ellen, though he didn't think so at the time. He yawned. It was time to pray and go to sleep. Tonight he didn't get too far on the prayers, but he didn't know because he was sleeping.

It was two thirty in the morning when they heard a child's cry. Both sit straight up in bed.

"What is that?" Andrew was startled. "Isn't Andy at Harriet's?" Anne was pushing off the side of the bed, in an extreme hurry.

He followed her into the guest room. Light flooded the room when she flipped the switch. Sitting up in the bed Andy had just given up was a little blonde haired blue eyed girl, tears running down her cheek and her thumb in her mouth.

"Whose baby is this?" He watched as Anne brought her out of the bed and the little girl wrap her arms around Anne's neck. The snubbing that wracked her body began to ease. All he could do was follow Anne back to their bedroom where she sit on the edge of the bed, rocking and crooning to the girl "Anne?" Something inside his mind was blocking out the anxiety he'd felt hearing her cry. Now he wanted to comfort her. He sit down by Anne. "Who is this? Does she have a name?"

Anne's cheek was to hers. "Adeline Grace. She's not two years old yet, but she can say her name and how old she is and she's probably hungry because she's been asleep through dinner."

"Hi, Adeline Grace." Andrew let her curl her finger around his. "I bet you don't give up that thumb, do you?" Adeline hic-cupped. "So where did you get her? Which of our friends does she belong to and are they sick?" He was scratching his head. "It's not every night I come home and there's a little girl in our bed."

"I didn't know what else to do, Andrew. Her mother is very ill and can't take care of her, she ask me if we would."

"We?" Andrew became reflective. "Watching Dan and Ellen, not to mention Marigold and Matt, caring for little ones' is a full time job. I had Andy a lot of the time, but I always had help," suddenly it came back to him. "I mistreated you during that time, Anne, I'm sorry."

She was silent, wondering should she just blurt it out or ease into the subject.

"Okay, I know she's not a figment of my imagination, nor a miracle birth, so tell me about Adeline Grace."

"I don't have more to tell. There's papers in the diaper bag, although I don't think she is still in diapers."

"I'll get the bag." Andrew found it by the bedroom door. "These papers?" Anne nodded. "Let's lay back on the bed, maybe she will go back to sleep." Getting situated, scooting in as close to Anne as she could, Adeline kept her eyes on him. Andrew opened the papers, one a letter, and began to read, his face turning red the farther he read and his hands beginning to shake. "This can't be. She's Summer's child?" He was upright in the bed, digging farther into the bag, finding the photo album and opening it. "I don't believe it. Is she trying to pawn one of her mistake onto us?" He climbed off the bed and began to pace. "Do you believe this…this…propaganda she's written down? That I fathered this child? Do you?"

"Andrew," Anne said, softly. "Bring the picture of you as a baby from Andy's room; Just bring his, too." Andrew gave her a disbeliev-ing look and walked across the hall to Andy's room. Bringing back both pictures he sat down, once more on the edge of the bed, but handed Anne the photos. Sitting up, Anne pulled Adeline next to her body and held Andrew's picture by Adeline's face. "Now you tell me, is Summer trying to pawn this little one off on us? Or, does she belong with us because you are her father?"

It seemed an eternity Andrew studied the picture, then the little girl, at last his eyes coming to rest on Adeline. Tears welled up in his eyes, his lip trembled and he was hoarse when he spoke. "I didn't know. Why didn't she tell me?"

"What did the letter say? I suspect she was angry, hurt and disillusioned, we remarried and it was awhile before she realized she was pregnant with your child. I'm just telling you how I felt when you left me." Anne sighed. "I was never sure you wanted to do the right thing or if you thought it would save you from going to prison. My life was in turmoil and having to do everything, meet bills and go to school was almost more than I could handle, if it hadn't been for Ellen I wouldn't have made it."

He covered his face with his hands, sitting bent on the edge of the bed, folded up as though he were hurting. "I cannot believe this. You would take in Summer's child, after the way she hurt you?"

"I brought home your child, because her mother is dying of cancer and she has no place to go. If you are the father and it looks to me you are, would you reject your own child? And it's true, you hurt me, Andrew, you took our son and kept him from me and laughed while you were doing it. You paraded women in front of me, denied money that I needed that would've helped me acquire an education and only by the grace of God I lived through the terrible accident." He was crying, but she finished, "I'll not say a word of this again, but yes, I brought home Andrew Graves child because her mother is dying."

The torment played out on his features. "I'm sorry." He seemed not to know what to do. Anne felt numb watching him, she hadn't meant to torment him, knowing he had changed and they were building a life together under God's umbrella. Quiet, holding Adeline Grace to her body, comforted by the little one looking up occasionally to her with those trusting eyes they watched him pace until he was worn through and sank back onto the bed. With his head on the pillow the cries abating, his breathing became steady as he lay there staring at the ceiling. It was then, Adeline moved from Anne's lap, crawled over to Andrew and snuggled into the curve of his arm.

Surprised but pleased, Anne turned off the light, returned to her side of the bed and pulled the sheet over the three of them. There were no words uttered. None were needed.

* * * * * * * *

Daniel had tossed and turned most of the night. In the early morning hours he turned the light on in the kitchen and made coffee. In his hand was the card given to him by Stephen Silvi. "Call me any hour," the man said. "Now, he kept thinking of something from Walden's speech the night of the ball. "When you least expect me, I will be there, when I've made a plan, no man can break it because I serve a higher power. There are none you can hold from me, when the time arrives, you will see, in the flash of lightening hitting the ground, I will have gathered my candidates and they will not be found." Daniel glanced at the phone; did he dare call the man at this early hour? Picking up the phone, he dialed.

Silvi answered on the first ring. "Good morning," he said. "I hoped you would call."

"Why's that?"

"Something was troubling you that you would not share in the meeting. I puzzled over this a good part of the night and finally decided it must relate to your family. Men are reluctant to share personal things."

"Is it common for someone like Walden to speak in rhymes?

Not the best of rhyming, but still…" Pausing, to assimilate his words, Daniel continued, "I don't know what his words mean, nor to whom they are aimed. I'll read to you what was written down."

Listening, when Daniel finished, Silvi said. "Consider this; Walden was an influential figure In your community. He is highly intelligent, or was; he began to use the drugs thinking they would increase his awareness and whatever situation he faced he would be ahead of his opponent. But the drugs ruined everything, still he didn't quit, even after losing his wife, one of the richest women in the city. In time he lost his business. He was on the run from the Cartel, and yet he continued to fall deeper into the web of his own creation. Walden believes he is invincible. He thinks he cannot be defeated."

"He should know by now." Daniel felt helpless to understand how Walden's mind worked. "He's on the run, and doesn't know it. He will be caught? Is that what you are thinking?"

"Partly," Silvi agreed, "but the most worrisome aspect of this situation is he is out to hurt someone, and he very well might do just that. He could also destroy more than we've discussed. What we are trying to do is unravel the words he spouts, rhyming words sometimes. I, alone, met with you but my colleagues were dissecting the dialogue he gave at the Ball and the Day in the Park. I don't know if it's possible he has sold his soul to the devil, one thing is for certain he does not serve your God."

"How do you know about my God? The other thing I want to know is what you're not telling us."

On the other end of the line, Silvi grew momentarily quiet. "In your garden, my friend, a dear lady and your little daughter Ruthie tried to explain to me the God you serve. The dear lady has withdrawn from our relationship of being friends and yet I know, she loves your Lord. What I have found in your group of believers is this, you lead by how you live your lives and it is quite obvious, unlike

Walden, your people serve a risen Savior. Never before have I seen such loyalty to one another and your God."

"You humble me, Silvi. We are only soldiers trying to do our best, but sadly sometimes we fail." Daniel glanced out the window. "A new day has dawned. Do you have the plan for his capture secured?"

"My friend, you may fail, but according to Miss Suze you ask forgiveness and there's the difference." Stephen Silvi paused, allowing the line to go quiet.

"What are you holding back from us, Silvi? It is our family's lives on the line. Tell me." There was only silence. "This is beyond our understanding. Surely you understand our concern."

"Set up a meeting, Daniel and we will confirm our latest plans with the others." The line went dead.

Anne and Andrew

Anne waited, though she had been awake hours. Now she felt she must call Summer. She dialed.

"May I speak with Summer?" Her shoulders drooped. "When did this happen?" She listened. "Did the soldier stay long? You didn't meet him? He drove Summer home. Yes, I have Adeline. Oh, you knew?"

Andrew came into the kitchen. Anne turned to him. "Summer died last night, actually three in the morning. She had told her neighbors and the people from Hospice about us and that Adeline was your child and would be coming to live with us. They will stand with us as Summer wished, if needed."

"How could she know you would agree?"

"She told them over a month ago, when she had the papers drawn up and completed. She told them we were the best people in the world and Adeline would be happy and content with us." Anne sit down at the table, lay her head on her arms and sobbed. "How could anyone think we were that good, Andrew?" Stepping behind her, Andrew put his arms around her shoulders. She felt his tears.

"You are that good, Anne. You've always been kind and considerate and Summer saw the way you loved our boy."

"But she gave us her baby."

"I know," he soothed. "You must have agreed to take her when you brought her home last night. Did you?"

Anne felt a pat-pat on her knee and raising her head found Adeline looking up at her. Gathering the child into her arms and to her body, she gave a strangled sob mixed with laughter. "How could I not?"

Later as they sit drinking coffee and watching Adeline eat scrambled eggs, Andrew turned on the television. "Today we honor our fallen soldiers," the anchor was saying. Andrew heard Anne gasp. "That's him, Andrew. He's the soldier helped us and drove Summer home, except the lady at Summer's house said there was no soldier but Summer was at peace and had talked to someone until she died."

Chapter Eighteen

The Gates House

"The only way to reach Matt is to go to the hospital. Evidently he has forgotten our meeting."

Ellen nodded, agreeing. "I think seeing Marigold practically going through what happened with M.J. was a wakeup call for Matt. It was scary and I'm thinking we don't know what was going on until the doctor tells us. I wish I could go with you."

Ruthie overheard from where she was studying at the dining room table. "Momma, little Maggie had problems but remember when we put our arms around each other and hugged Marigold? That's the moment when everyone was praying and right then God healed her. It will be on the doctor's record.

Marigold and Daniel stared at their daughter. "Healing?" They said in unison.

"Something like that."

"In view of a possible problem and Marigold needing her husband, why do you need Matt?"

"We need him to finalize the plans concerning Walden. It's going to take meticulous timing and if he fails to bring the device he stole from the government we may not be able to pull it off. It's like an illusion. Now you see it, then you don't. If Stephen Silvi hadn't known about it, we wouldn't have a clue."

"This gets stranger and stranger." Ellen drew in a deep breath. Please don't get hurt." She started to walk into the other room, but turned back. "I have two questions. One, so Ruthie and I will understand; explain the device, this is beginning to sound like a science fiction movie and number two, do you trust this man sent to help you? Could he be on Walden's side?"

Dan blew out a big breath, "it's not that we haven't considered this. He is so different. Andrew checked him out. Washington agreed there's endless data racked up behind his name. He is the expert on a man reaching a certain level in life when something goes haywire. In Pookie's case, he was besieged by Walden's ruthless charm; no way knowing who the man was he was speaking with. Britany being his wife and seemingly under Walden's spell has additional influence on Pookie. He truly loves her and would do anything for her, whether she loves him is another thing entirely."

"This is so far out of the realm of what we are used to, Daniel. Have you found anything in scripture that relates to this?"

"We wrestle not against flesh and blood but against principalities, against power, against the rulers of darkness of this world, found in Ephesians," Dan quoted. "As we understand Walden as a child lived in a strange environment, one we can't imagine, his parents died and he was raised by a grandmother that practiced a different religion than any we recognize, then he found the drug business lucrative which meant he left behind his law practice, his wife divorced him when he had an affair with her daughter and that cut off his plan to run for Congress and from there who knows what he would have done. At one time he had great Charisma, but by his own hand he used drugs which impaired his mentality. What seems far out to us was reality to him and he began to think he had supernatural powers."

"It seems he was scorned after the affair with his step daughter and yet, anything I've read he has a great magnetism and people are drawn to him," Ellen sank onto the arm of Dan's chair. "I'm sure your committee read all the material I've read, but what is this black box thing?"

Daniel shook his head, "I don't know if there is a black box or if that's what someone named it, it may be what Walden calls it. I'm also unsure how Walden came into possession or knowledge of something completely unknown to the average citizen or how that could happen. The biggest fear is that someone uses it and the entire grid is disrupted. Silvi explained countries must avoid the collapse of its system, think of transportation, air and land, consider computers, not your personal computer only but those that track security for our country or on a smaller scale to our community's safety. We're dealing with things we don't understand."

"Have there been incidents recorded in our country?"

"That's why he and his colleagues are sent out when they receive word as to illegal use. The government keeps it hush hush for security reasons, no doubt, but also to prevent panic. It isn't easy to discern something that's invisible but the results of use are visible such as when a railway is hit, or airlines close down or utilities in a city the size of New York shut down."

"Invisible hacking," Ellen offered. "And we thought Walden was dangerous because he suffers mentally and is cruel. Now we find he is a self-employed espionage agent and possibly doesn't even know it. Why hasn't our government got involved in this? I'm confused, is this a cyber attack?"

Dan smiled. Ellen took a deep breath, "I meant on a larger scale than what you've just told me."

"Remember the men we met with secretly? If the public knew, pandemonium might break loose."

"It's scary. I'm beginning to see why he thinks he's invincible, that no one can touch him, but Dan are these Federal agents or merely men employed by the government because of their expertise?"

"Does it matter as long as they know what they are doing? The one comes across as knowledgeable." Worry crossed his brow. "I've got to find Matt." Daniel's glance roamed the room. "Kiss our babies and keep the door locked. Who knows where he will show up? His brain is not functioning. Whether what we've been told is true or not, he is a hurting individual. Now we have to find what his next plan holds for us."

* * * * * * * *

The hospital staff was busy with changeover, the night shift listening to what the day personnel offered on each patient. Daniel took the elevator to third floor and found Marigold's room. She was holding a baby wrapped in a striped blanket, with a lot of black hair and a tiny pink bow on the very top.

Marigold's eyes lit up with pleasure as she put a finger to her lips and motioned for Daniel to look to the corner where Matt was sound asleep in a hospital recliner.'

"Does he snore?" He whispered.

"I think he's too tired to snore." The smile disappeared, replaced by a serious expression. "He's told me about Walden. Do you need Matt?" Dan nodded. "Are you guys careful, Dan? I'm in no shape to lose my husband or a friend."

"How's the baby?"

"Did Ruthie tell you anything, Dan?"

"Only that prayer changes things, but we all know that to be true."

"The doctor said when our little girl," She smiled and corrected, "When Maggie was born. There was a problem. The doctor said he massaged her heart and it began a regular beat, but there was a time he and the attending nurse thought they'd lost her. It was a God thing he said, a higher power, because the time she was lifeless was already being charted. I ask him what time and Dan, it was the same hour Ruthie felt the need to come see me, and even when they brought Maggie into the room, they were concerned but they wanted me to hold her while she was breathing. Ruthie put her arms around me," Marigold began to weep, but continued in a soft voice, "And Ellen put her arms around both of us and Matt…Matt was so upset, he was holding me from the side, his big old arms around us…oh, Dan, it was such a strong powerful moment, the Spirit of the Lord came down, touched our baby…and we knew." A sob escaped in the form of half laughter from Marigold's lips, and then our Ruthie said, "We can go home now."

Dan's eyes filled with tears. "I didn't know. That explains the quiet I've felt in Ruthie and Ellen. When the Lord allows a moment like you experienced, our spirit is so near to Him, we are so washed in his power we savor it, and save it until we feel we can share it."

They were quiet for a while. "I'm glad you shared that now, Marigold. I needed it. This episode with Walden has been ten times worse than what we experienced when he tied his own cousin to the old farm house post and left him to die. I've almost felt it was some charade pressed upon us and there was no way out. It has helped me considerably to know the Holy Spirit visited you in this room."

"It has been evil, hasn't it, Dan?" Marigold glanced at her sleeping husband. "We get ourselves into such depth of misery, ours was being separated but Matt felt he had to help his parents and I tried to be brave and go on, like a soldier's wife must, but inside my heart was breaking not only because he was gone but because his parents have no use for me or our children and I can't understand what I've done, because I've not been given a chance to do anything. Walden let himself get pulled into many things, too."

"The difference, Marigold, is he had a choice. He made cold hearted decisions based on greed and he's not finished. Right now he has a plan to destroy either a number of us or a whole town."

"Matt said the government has brought in an agent, do you approve?"

"I'm of mixed opinion, Marigold. When the government is involved, we are never certain, there's that item of truth and keeping it from the regular citizen on any different situation or level…I don't know."

"Do you wonder how you were brought in on this, Dan? It all started in his home town, didn't it, In Newhaven? That's what I understood when I was helping restore Shining Light Church after the fire."

"Another incident that proves God is in control of our lives. We've met fine people from Newhaven, but Walden was an active citizen here in the Cape, too. Andrew working for him shed light on Walden, we might not have had, otherwise."

Matt groaned, waking up, stretching his arms in the air. Daniel reached over to grab a hand. "It's about time, old friend. I thought we were going to have to wake you from your beauty nap. So kiss your bride, your little one and let's get going." He threw a kiss to Marigold,"Sorry, sister, got'ta take your man."

"Do we have any idea, whatsoever, what we are getting ourselves in to? I mean, this is far out, man."

"I hear you," Dan replied, "but what are our options? It's our families at risk. You and I don't think he has powers but what if he does? Aren't bad attitudes and a desire to hurt others an opposite of love thy neighbor as thyself?" He glanced over to Matt and saw him nod. "That is a dark spirit. Not of God. Then who takes pleasure in that kind of thinking?"

Matt kissed Marigold. "Don't worry, Tinkerbell, I'll be back.

* * * * *

Climbing into Dan's work van, Matt confessed, "I'm uneasy about what might happen."

"We all are." Dan drove by the complex where they were supposed to meet. "Do you see anything that tips you off as not being right?"

Matt studied the place. "Only that Silvi guys black Suburban's available."

"Matt," Daniel glanced his way, their eyes holding for a minute. "Is it possible our earth, today, right now as we speak, is so filled with the things of the devil that our God is watching us, giving us an opportunity to correct the filth we allow and we are standing in the brink, waiting to be held accountable?"

"That gives me goose bumps to think everything could get so involved. I thought we were looking for a man whose mind is ruined by drugs, a man who could hurt himself as easily as he can hurt us."

"Think how many have turned away from the Lord. Many churches have empty pews Sunday after Sunday. Think about our country, the news issued daily and there's always someone trying to prove only Heaven knows what, and we know that's only the tip of the iceberg."

"You're saying Silvi, or Walden or Joe on the corner has to start listening, less we all perish."

They were walking in, when Matt remembered. "Marigold gave me orders to message Leah Merkal that our baby arrived, but I don't have their email address, do you?"

Shining Light Church

The Sewing Club was in full swing. Leah was in the office with Levi when Suze Norman entered.

"Is it all right if I come in to run off papers for the sewing girls? Am I interrupting a private meeting?"

"No, everything's fine. I just received a message from Daniel Graves, remember the couple who led singing in our Spring Revival? Well, he says our designer; Mrs. Marigold Langley has delivered a seven pound baby girl with a head full of black hair like her Momma and Daddy's doing well, also."

Leah was clapping her hands. "Yay, for Marigold. I'm next." She grabbed Suze and did a little circle dance, then hugged her profusely and said, "I'm so happy everything went well for Marigold and baby."

"There's more." Levi's expression clouded as he read, "We are inviting you, Pastor Merkal to join us tonight as we work against the forces of evil. Bring only your Bible."

"Something's going on there," Suze said. "I hear it involves Clayton Walden. I wondered if there was anything to it. When we were young, if Clayton or Herm were involved it was trouble all the way."

Levi and Leah exchanged glances. "Kind of like trouble times two, huh?" Levi questioned.

"Talulah can tell you a head full," Suze replied. "There were times we wondered if those two were spawned by the devil but then again, there was their grandmother as large as life in their background."

"I'll ride with you if you attend their meeting," Leah offered. "Would you like to go, Suze?"

Tears sprang into Suze eyes. "No one ever asks me to go anywhere, how graciously kind of you."

"What time?" Leah closed in on Levi sitting thinking. "I know you are checking our church schedule in your mind and I don't believe you will find a thing for tonight. So what time?" She grinned, foolishly pleased to think of seeing a new born baby and spending time with Marigold even in a hospital.

"Could we leave in an hour and stop at Lucy's diner for a plate of chicken and dumplins?" Now he was grinning. "It will be my treat, Suze, how about it?"

Suze checked her watch. "I'll deliver these papers and head on home. Can you pick me up there?" She was almost through the door when she turned."Thank you so much for inviting me along." The door closed behind her. Talulah Cohen was sitting at her desk, a speculative expression on her face. "Is there something going on in there I should know about? I am the secretary."

Suze stopped dead in her tracks. "Remember Mrs. Marigold Langley? She's had her baby." Suze smiled. "Pastor Levi and Mrs. Leah are going to the hospital to visit and invited me to come along."

Andrew and Anne Graves

Andrew had missed a lot of sleep. A meeting was planned for the night, after ten o'clock. An hour most respectable people would be readying for bed but those hyped up with energy, like Walden, might be roaming the streets, invisible or possibly thinking they were flying. He thought he had seen Walden in his back yard last night and while it gave him cold chills and made his heart race, he realized it was all part of Walden's plan. Andrew shook off the feeling of dread; the alarm system worked, he had the gun hidden within his reach but not little Andy's. For now, he wanted to surprise Anne and the children.

Children. It pleased him to say the word, to think it. Little Andy was now big brother to Adeline. Tomorrow at eleven o'clock, his family would join friends and family of Summer Wheaton to observe the last memorial to her life. A sense of sadness crossed his heart. It was never planned to his benefit, to have the little girl he had not known until two days ago. He could not deny she was his child, a child he would fight the courts and any blood kinsman to Summer Wheaton, to keep, whether appointed as her guardian or legal parent. He was Adeline Grace's father.

Anne came to mind. Sweet Anne had brought home his love child when the birth mother could no longer keep her; Adeline's mother was dying of cancer and passed the very first night Adeline was with them. He had to thank Anne for her willingness to take another woman's child. Already she picked up Adeline, crooning, whispering mother and child love notes to his daughter by another woman. She was one in a million. He made his way into the Shoppe touting a sign that read *treasures for all.* "Do you have clothing for women and children?"

"What did you have in mind, Sir?"

"A beautiful dress in size six for my wife, suitable for church, and a frilly little frock for a two year old," He replied, "Then there's my son four, going on five. We all need to match because it's a special day and we want to be appropriately dressed; whatever it takes to please the eye, shoes, socks, the works."

"We will do our best, sir. How do you feel about navy?"

"That sounds a little dark, doesn't it?"

"Not for special occasion and this time of year, sir." She led the way. "This little dress would be beautiful on a child of any coloring, hair, eyes, you understand?"

"She's a blonde." They all are my wife, my daughter, my son." He smiled as it rolled off his tongue.

He left the store three hundred eighty dollars less in his account than when he entered but there was a tie in the box to go with the light blue shirt and Navy sport coat he already owned. He would recall that day and his little excursion many times over in the years to come and it would read like a paragraph all joined together, because that's the way it was. "You've done well," the lady said. He replied, "So have you." He felt happy. Carrying in the box, he called to Anne. "Hon, I've never done this before. I hope you won't feel bad about it." He placed the boxes on the bed in their room, and looked in on his sleeping children. Anne's laughter was as clear and sweet as a bell. "You have changed." Arms around his neck she kissed him. "How did you know what size shoe Andy wears?" He grinned. "I sneaked a peak this morning of his tennis shoes and got a half size larger, hers too." She kissed him again. "You did well, Mr. Lawyer. Now let's see what you have for Adeline." She savored opening the box with Adeline's items, slowly examining each piece and when finished put her arms around his neck, nose to nose, eye to eye and smiled. Andrew felt like a million dollars. "I should do this often," he said, "when we have more money." The largest box containing her dress, a silver bracelet with a pearl and his tie were last. There were tears in her eyes. "It's a sad occasion for Adeline," she said, "but you have given us a nice memory. We will never forget this." She held the dress to her body. "It looks perfect."

"There's a meeting tonight at ten." Their eyes met. "I want you to keep the alarm on; don't open the door to anyone. We plan to be in our homes by twelve but these are the final plans, as the Silvi guy called it our final briefing. He's military too, I suppose; for now he's been hired by our government."

* * * * * * * *

A casual drive by, Walden thought, scanning the street, there where the Graves lived, on to the old rich lady's home. He'd take that fat Hattie too, but she was too much to wrestle if she wouldn't come peacefully. He had to think of everything. He had the information he needed on the gifted girl, there was a baby nearby, he'd see how that went. One by one, he lined them up, his victims, those poor nitwits who thought they were smarter than him, they were dumb. He had it all figured out. The place to abandon them was difficult but he hired a helicopter, manned by a cold hearted son of the devil who had no qualms when he told them the planned demise. "Just be sure there are two men on the platform to receive them. No last minute hitch; when we start we push it through all the way."

His heart lurched inside his chest. Perhaps he'd taken to much medicine. He had to have a clear mind. There was no wind; there would be no problem with the helicopter. "Remember," he'd cautioned in return, "the last thing you are to do is bring my men back down to ground level."

"Collect your package at eleven," he instructed the men. "One at a time go to your pick up spot at precisely the hour you have been appointed and once your package is in the helicopter, you disappear unless you are designated to go up with the package."

"When the last package is dropped inside the retainer, our man will seal the door. Don't let yourself be locked inside nor stranded on the platform. Once the door is closed, it will not be reopened. That's our instruction. Your money is in the mail. I hope we never see each other again."

He drove by the complex. There they were, smart as all rookies, completely visible through the window, sitting at the table, their important papers before them. Graves, Gates, Langley, Gipson, the two ministers and the man from the FBI. He laughed. They were worried because he had the upper hand. They had no idea how far above their mentality he had climbed. He listened to them, now.

Ah, the wonders of modern technology, especially when he was privy to such.

Inside, Silvi apologized to the ministers. "I'm sorry to disturb your evening but we may need your expertise in this endeavor. If Walden is operating on a demonical base, we need you to counter his act."

It was good of Gates to invite the two ladies to his home. "I'm sure they will spend a pleasant evening with Miss Ellen. We have instructed their needs be met for a comfortable night's stay in the Cape."

Silvi motioned to Harper Gipson, as planned a crackling noise enveloped the room. "The equipment seems to be running smoothly. An interceptor prevents those with high tech machines outside this building, from hearing our conversation. Now," he unrolled a map, placed it on the wall cork board. These are the places we feel most likely Walden has scouted out, for the big delivery he's planning that in his mind will make us all sit up and take notice."

"What is the big delivery?" Levi asked. "I'm just coming on board and no one's had time to fill me in."

Grim faced, Silvi drew a deep breath and expelled before explaining. "We believe in this room we are all united but that's not necessarily true in Walden's camp. One of his big burly men became too intoxicated for his own good, last night. He mentioned Walden and his crew plan a pick up and drop plan for tonight's work."

"What is it?" Levi was leaning forward, interested. "Chemicals? Maybe for City Hall."

"No. Kidnapping of various family members; that's the pick-up, the most important aspect of this project. Today we visited every place where Walden might be interested in leaving his cargo. The last on our list is most likely his first choice.. You notice he's using common terms, lest someone is listening."

"Cut to the chase, man." Matt spoke up. "Where is it?"

"The cargo, called his pick-up, turns out to be some of our own people and the place of drop is the water tower."

Gipson whistled. "That's fifty feet up. How does he plan to achieve that little feat? Filling it with water began this evening at six o'clock. By morning the doors will be sealed."

"Excuse me." Levi had a picture forming in his head and he was beginning to feel the heat. "What are the doors used for?"

"It's not an actual door; it's a panel, two panels, in fact they were removed for cleaning before the filling. Someone will have to…"

"Excuse me," Levi was calculating the circumference of the water tower. "I'm sorry I was gathering info… "They'll have to use a helicopter, for sure and a good pilot."

"He hasn't dropped them in yet," Joe began. "But knowing his history, he will. Someone will have…"

Matt's face settled into granite. "I'll do it," he said. "I'll go up to stay with them when they're dropped. Walden plans to seal them in if they don't drown first. Lord have mercy on us if there is such a device. That's just another thing to work with and frankly, I'm nearing my wits end."

"It's not every day citizens work with an electo magnetic device. The government admits one is missing and Walden was in the area at the time it went missing, but does he have training of use? No." Silvi's expression was grim.

At The Gates House

"I'm embarrassed," Suze offered. "Am I intruding on your hospitality? There was no way I knew we would be staying over. I don't have so much as a tooth brush."

Ellen touched Suze arm. "It doesn't matter. There are new ones in the guest bathroom. I have clean gown and robes for both of you. And Suze, this may be a strange way to welcome you into our midst but God has a hand in it or it would never have happened, so please, put your mind at ease."

"I'm afraid I don't understand what this is all about, other than Clayton Walden and he was always trouble." She settled into one of the rocking chairs. "You may know by now, Clayton has a strange desire to hurt people. If we are smart, we in Newhaven stay out of his path."

"But it's impossible to do that, here in the Cape, when he is vindictive because he lost his family and his business when he went to jail." Ellen was sitting on the edge of the sofa arm as Leah came into the room wearing one of her robes, smiling and clean, doing a little plie' before taking the other rocker.

"Did I miss something?" She smiled again, her dimples deepening. "I must say this is a treat, staying in your beautiful home, Ellen. We ate chicken and dumplings at Lucy's, visited Marigold and saw her precious little baby girl…and here we are. It's like vacation all rolled into one."

Ellen laughed. "With two sets of twins, it's always bedlam getting everyone settled, you also witnessed that."

"I don't know how you do it." Leah gave Suze a glance. "I worry whether I'll measure up as a mommie or a pastor's wife when our baby arrives."

Suze leaned forward. "You know I'll never have a grandchild, if I could help you, Leah, I'm happy to offer myself. I've never repeatedly rocked a baby to sleep, you know what I mean, but then as long as Wade was here I never missed it too much, though there were times I yearned for it."

"I'm sure you ladies are tired; let me show you where things are in your rooms, give you a flashlight in case the power should go off and we'll turn in for the night. Wherever the men are they are together and that is more comforting than if they were each alone."

Leah wrinkled her nose, "I don't think we'll need the flashlights, there's no weather on the forecast. There's more to the meeting our men are in than I'm aware of, isn't there, Ellen?"

"I'm afraid so." She sighed. "It would not hurt if we three prayed for our men, our world as we know it. Now," she glanced from one to the other, "who wants to pray?" Suze and Leah pointed to her.

"Where's Ruthie?" Leah asked, glancing down the hall.

"She was worn out after helping me with the twins. My swee-tums is asleep in her bed."

Ellen read from the Bible,"Ephesians Six, twelve. We wrestle not against flesh and blood but against principalities, against power, and against the rulers of darkness of this world." Then she prayed.

"Our Lord and Heavenly Father, we come with grateful hearts. Lord forgive us our sins that we might pray for others, for the safety of our husbands, friends and our world that has been drawn into conflict. We, Lord, do not understand the entanglements of worldly things that would bring hurt whether physically or emotionally to others, but we ask your divine attendance to the matters others would bring upon our lives. We praise you Lord, when we feel weak, defeated and alone in dark situations not of our doing but that hap-pen in our midst. We ask protection on those who must wage the war against the principalities your scripture speaks of, the power of people in high places and the ruler of darkness that walks our earth shattering lives. But we know, Lord, where there's destruction you rebuild, where there's heartache you bring peace and through your love Lord, we can walk through valleys and find the mountaintop you have in store for us. We love you Lord. We ask you to watch over our loved ones, our friends and those Lord who have no one at all. For it is in your gracious and holy name we pray. Amen."

"Come Lord Jesus, Come," Leah whispered. "I feel the presence of the Lord is with us, Ellen."

"It has been many years since I've felt God's glory touch my soul, Ellen, as now." Suze realized there were tears in her eyes as well as theirs. "What is happening, Ellen, that the Lord has blessed us tonight in your home."

Clasping the Bible to her chest, Ellen shook her head. "I don't know. When the devil walks across our lives and we pray from our hearts, God touches us. Where two or more agree together, He is present. And if there are times we are alone, the Holy Spirit joins us and prays with us. I believe. Do you believe?"

"I have this feeling, Ellen, we are not meant to retire to our beds, but to keep vigil through the night."

"I agree, Leah. How do you feel, Suze?"

"There are few times in life I've felt the Holy Spirit this strong. To leave this place of Holiness would be wrong. If we tire and go to sleep, I feel it will be all right, but for now to sit quietly and think on the Lord and pray seems to be what we are to do. Forgive my boldness; it would be wrong if I said other."

"Then I will lower the light and we will agree together. It is not ours to know why, but to leave to the Lord what will be done. If we are here at sunrise, that is good. It is where we were meant to be."

Chapter Nineteen

Matt began the climb, up the ladder, the safety chain moving forward, above him one step at a time. It was imperative he start now. If what Silvi said was true, word had come from the man in custody that Walden was intending to shut down the town tonight, he must be ready on the platform to help those Walden's men would be dropping into the water tower's holding tank by way of helicopter. The situation was unreal. He thought on that as he struggled in the dark, no light, no helicopter for him, only the prayers that went before him by the men below and he prayed those God would waken from sleep knowing something was wrong and as a warrior for their Lord know it was time to pray.

Could one man's hatred of others bring such chaos? How had Walden obtained the necessary tool to bring destruction to the Cape and possibly the territory beyond in his ignorance of what he held in his hands? Was he so far gone by way of the drugs he did not realize it would kill him too? Or was it the demonic entity that held him in bonds he had not yet discovered, strangling him, demanding he do the satanic work his mind toyed with day to day but lacked the courage to act upon because it was an evil even he in his twisted mind could not imagine?

When did one, such as he, Matt Langley put aside personal distrust and pray for a man who had taken on the guise of the devil, lowered himself to crawling on his knees, and thinking he could fly through the air when he was at the highest level of his utopia, his own self-made paradise that had destroyed many good men trying to forget the deception life had made of their soul? Matt had known good men who went to war, returning lost souls seeking help for acts committed who found no peace and turned the other direction. Oh, God, he prayed, be in this tonight. For our tiny little corner of the world, Lord, relieve us of the consequence of one man's distorted mind. In the darkness, climbing upward the scripture from Phillipians came to him. Aloud, as he climbed, Matt repeated it over and over. "Do not be anxious about anything," he quoted, "but in every situation, by prayer and petition, with thanksgiving, present your requests to God, and the peace of God, which transcends all understanding, will guard your hearts and your minds in Christ Jesus." He slid into place. In the dark, waiting. He was ready.

* * * * * * *

"What do you mean you were unable to breach the Gates home? It is vital we have a gifted child. This is our opportunity to change the world." Walden's man remained firm. "There's a field of protection around that home. You want the girl. Come get her." Transmission broke. Walden moved on.

"Do you have the baby?" His laughter thundered. "Now we have the old lady, yes, the rich one." Then his tone changed, was it remorse or anger held at bay. "Who said she died? Bring her body?

You don't tell me no, I own you. Bring her that I may see." But the worker had heard the first man. "You want her," he said, "Come get her yourself, I will not trespass the dead." The second radio failed.

Walden's anger reached scale. Only the approach of the helicopter stopped him from pushing the button on the strange apparatus he had in his possession. "It will shut down power," his benefactor said. "Be certain what you do is what you want. There's no turning back." He watched. The men in the complex had gone home, the building was black, not a light in the inner office. He saw the first one dropped from the helicopter, the old lady. Your riches didn't help you this time, did they? But the second body was a man. He had not ordered any man be dropped into the tower's depth. His anger rose again. Now, a woman holding a baby, would her presence replace the need for the gifted child? She was not without sin. No. Drop her, he commanded, "No," the voice from the helicopter replied. "She carries the child." I said drop her. Slowly, the man lowered the helicopter and the woman and child disappeared. "Leave. There are no men to rescue, they abandoned me for a time, but they will return." The helicopter rose into the air, the blades filling the air with a whump-whump sound.

"It's time to push the button, let the world go black. You have redeemed yourself," the demons of his soul cried out, but Walden felt bands of steel wrap around his body, squeezing, squeezing until he felt nothing but blessed night. He had accomplished what he set out to do. Grandmother would be proud of him. Now he was back in her yard. She beckoned. Come to me, Clayton and bring Herm with you."

Light came on the tower, surrounded it, and flooded every inch where the workmen had need. Matt hurried, lowered himself into the depth and darkness. The missing panels allowed him enough light to see the woman, a huddled figure holding the baby to her breast, protecting it from the water he had not been able to lower. In the dark he was helpless to know where every line was placed.

"Matt. Matt?" It was Harriet's voice. "Matt." Thanksgiving and praise all in one. "Praise God."

"Not for me Harriet, to our Lord. Now, let's get you out of here." The man was helping. "Walden's plans went astray," he said. "At last minute his men refused to do his dirty work. There were others intended, but your Lord heard the prayers of many and threw up a shield."

"My Lord? Yes. Yes, I'm sure He did." Matt was startled to find Silvi the one helping with the rescue. "How did you get to the top so fast?"

"It is not so difficult," Silvi replied, "if you find where the helicopter lands and grab hold as it leaves the ground." Silvi steadied Mrs. Becker as they were ready to climb the make shift ladder up through the panels. "Your friends have contact the proper channels to take the lady and baby back, we believe to the hospital. They have the police on standby."

"I wondered why they were not with us at all times."

"Too many would have alert Walden we were on to him. The FBI has first priority in this case."

Matt found the woman. She was in shock but would not allow removal of the baby. Her arms tightened around the baby. "No. No. No." She fought him off. Matt took a step back.

"Marigold?" She recognized his voice. She turned, the sheet falling from her body, the baby covered by a blanket. "Marigold."

She felt his arms around her. "Why, Matt? Why?" She shivered beneath the light hospital gown.

Matt clasp her to his chest. She seemed addled. No doubt Walden's goons had given her something to subdue her while they whisk her from the hospital floor. He knew in his heart Maggie was Marigold's first concern. He almost smiled except for the circumstance he faced of taking her and Maggie off the tower. Harriet, on the other hand was as alert as any given day. No doubt she gave them a struggle.

"There's an incoming helicopter," Silvi informed him. "It will carry the three of you and the baby. I will return to the ground on my own. Everything that has happened will be kept top-secret, Mr. Langley."

Hospital at the Cape

Truth hit home. Marigold was beside herself. She could not control the shaking of her body. She handed Maggie to Matt. Her teeth chattered as she ask, "Was it best we were here at the hospital, even if they lost us?" A nurse was busy wrapping her with a warm blanket while avoiding looking her in the eye. "They were not aware we were gone, Matt. What kind of security is that for a hospital?"

"You're all right, Babe. That's what matters. We all need to get some sleep. Look at this baby; she's sleeping right through it all." He noticed Harriet standing outside the room. They were both grinning.

"We go home, tomorrow, Matt. Will you stay with us?" She noticed the nurse took interest in her words. "He's a farmer," Marigold explained. "He has to leave us for harvest." The nurse scurried out of the room. "She better run." Marigold felt grumpy, the irritableness they'd thought to treat by giving her medication on her return needed to kick in. "If anything happened to my baby…"

Harriet came through the door. "Well, I've seen you in this mood one other time, when I came to see you and M.J. and you told me if I didn't intend to be a mother and grand ma I could just go home, you didn't need me."

"I haven't heard this story," Matt said, yawning and handing the baby over to Harriet. "What did you do?"

"Why, I stayed. I rocked M.J., cleaned the kitchen, washed about fifteen baby bottles it seemed and I didn't go home until she said I could. She was tired, her hair was standing on end and it was the day her milk came in and she was a mess, crying and mad because she couldn't get everything done."

"Where was I?"

Harriet was adoring her granddaughter. "That's a good question. I know you were at work but was it with Harper Gibson's construction company or were you helping on the farm then, too?" Relieved to see Marigold had crawled onto the bed and was already asleep, Matt yawned and motioned to Harriet to put the baby back in the bedside crib. "I'll take you home, Ma. I doubt Walden's men left you a car."

She gave him a disdainful glance. "I'm not your ma, so don't fill your oats with me, farm boy." She lay Maggie in the mini sized bed, "We're not leaving until they assure us someone's on security."

"I'll check."

The nurse in the hall, overheard. "Oh, yes sir. Some Federal Agent took care of that. That's why I'm here. I don't mean to be eaves dropping, but I'm to keep watch and alert them if anything's suspicious." She turned back the lapel of the jacket she wore over scrubs. "You see this little button like thing? All I got to do is press it and he assured me all hell would break loose. We won't lose your baby again." She gave the room a second look and added, "Nor your wife either. She sure wasn't happy, was she?"

The morning after

It was early morning when Daniel and Levi returned. They found the three women sitting at the kitchen table enjoying coffee. The twins were still asleep and Ruthie was joining the ladies as they arrived. Daniel noticed the fresh rolls, a stack of plates and cups on the counter; he hadn't eaten.

"Good morning, Ladies," placing a kiss on top of Ellen's head, he asked, "Did you have a nice rest?"

All three laughed. "In those wonderful relaxing chairs," Leah replied. "But we prayed most of the night." She noticed his surprise. "It seemed the thing to do, Daniel. You've heard the song Glory Came Down, haven't you? Well, we think glory came down, right here in your beautiful home."

"Not one bed has been disturbed," Ellen admitted. "Was your night productive?"

Together, Daniel and Levi told the story of their evening, "but the real shocker was when the woman and child turned out to be our Marigold and Maggie." Sipping coffee, he said, "That was something we least expected, right Joe?"

Ruthie sit quietly listening. "Are they all okay? I was awake last night praying for them and Andrew."

Daniel replied. "Andrew felt it best he go home to Anne and the children. The same with Joe."

"Children?" The four caught the word.

"Yes, Andrew and Annie have a new daughter. She is two years old and her name is Adeline Grace." His attention turned to Ellen, "If you are up to it, Ellen. Let's have everyone over tonight, that is if it works for Marigold and Matt, and we'll be sure Andrew and Annie's family are the center of attention."

"I can't believe you two were caught up in the middle of something so…so…dramatic. I'm at a loss for a word to describe it and you are as settled and cool as if nothing out of the ordinary happened."

"Levi and I discussed this," Daniel replied, "what used to be the norm, may not be anymore. Let's pray there aren't any other Walden figures running around out there to keep this kind of commotion going."

"It is scary," Levi admitted. "When a man has allowed himself to be involved in matters that are contrary not only to God's laws but to society's rules, someone is bound to be hurt. We are fortunate the person in charge was educated as to what could happen if not handled correctly." He addressed Daniel, "I understand you and the others, Gipson, Graves and Langley were none too positive about the Fed's man in charge, in the beginning."

"We were skeptical," Dan admitted, "but there comes a time you have to trust. He realized we weren't one hundred per cent sold on what he presented, but he handled himself so well we began to realize he had to answer to the pomp and circumstance of his calling, therefore it would hurt us only if we didn't work alongside him. We did and it turned out to our advantage. We have faith. I saw a glimmer of wanting our faith in this man but he's uncertain until he has his private life…well, that's his to tell."

"Does this man who orchestrated the capturing of poor demented Walden have a name?"

There was such a silence; Suze glanced quickly at Leah who was doing the same. "Maybe Suze and I should leave the room while you discuss the person."

"We'll just call him Mr. X if that's all right until we know if using his name would bring him harm. Is that fair enough?" Dan asked.

"I guess we exhausted that subject pretty quick, didn't we?" Leah's brows were raised, her eyes twinkling in merriment. "I think it's time we left our sweet hostess and be on our way. Are you ready Suze?" She went to Ellen and hugged her. "Thank you for loaning your home and your robe. I've thoroughly enjoyed time with you, though the circumstances were not ideal."

"Won't we see you tonight?"

"Sure," Leah winked, "and we'll all pretend we haven't seen each other today." The three laughed.

"Yes, thank you. The Spirit in your home is welcoming. I truly felt the love of God." Suze hugged Ellen.

As the last car left the drive, Dan shook his weary head. "No one could ever have made me believe what happened last night was real. How often does a man who has everything get caught up in greed and have the willingness to destroy lives as he endeavors to reach his own goal?

Glancing at Ellen, he thought he saw the weariness he was feeling in her. He had to be more careful that what was expected of him didn't lapse over into their family. "Are you tired, my love?" Dan's arms went around Ellen. "I worry about you. Did you get any rest?"

"Actually, we probably napped in our chairs more than we think, but we did pray a lot."

"And it was needed." Taking her hand he led her to the sofa in the adjoining room. "Did you know about Anne and Andrew's taking one of Andrew's acquaintance little daughter?" He continued. "It seems Adeline Grace belonged to Summer Wheaton, Walden's step daughter. You remember how badly Andrew treated Anne until she divorced him when he cast her aside for Summer? According to Andrew's explanation, Summer had been keeping an eye on Anne and when the cancer became last stage and Hospice was called in she realized it was time to give Adeline Grace to Anne." He sighed. "It's very sad. They are taking the children for eleven o'clock services for Summer's memorial, today."

It was Ellen's time to take Dan's hand and lead him to the bedroom. "I'll not tell the boys you are here, or they would not let you sleep. Now rest and I'll prepare for tonight when we celebrate Gods blessings. There could have been serious harm come to each of you. God granted mercy."

He didn't argue, but he handed her a card. "Do you mind? This is Stephen's number. He is almost persuaded, Ellen. He does not fully understand our commitment to our God, but his mind is searching as his heart cries out. There's something in his personal life needing closure. I don't know if it is something happened years ago or of late. You might ask him how he should be introduced." Dan sank onto the bed, giving a sigh of relief. "I'm sorry I can't help you right now, but if I can get a couple hours sleep…" She was draping the sheet around his shoulders. "Thank you, Ellen. I'm just about out on my feet. I called the office. Gene's taking care of things today." She was closing the door when she heard, "I love you."

Ellen made the call. "Mr. Silvi, my husband, Daniel Gates, ask that I call and invite you to a small gathering of friends, tonight, in our home. We would love to have you as our guest. I believe they will start arriving around six thirty. You are welcome. Oh, and Mr. Silvi, how are we to introduce you?"

She was filled with a desire to visit the angel in the flower garden. Ruthie was in her room preparing for another reading lesson with Angeline. The twins were still asleep. Ellen slipped quietly out into the back yard. Going to her favorite place she withdrew the Bible from beneath the seat of the bench placed in the shelter of the angel's spreading wings and as she opened it a light breeze rippled the pages. "Now Thomas, one of the twelve," she read, "was not with the disciples when Jesus came, so the other disciples told him, "We have seen the Lord." But he said to them, "Unless I see the nail marks in his hands and put my finger where the nails were, and put my hand into his side, I will not believe." A week later his disciples were in the house again and Thomas was with them. Though the doors were locked, Jesus came and stood among them and said, "Peace be unto you? Then he said to Thomas, "Put your finger here; see my hands. Reach out your hand and put it into my side. Stop doubting and believe." Thomas said to him, "My Lord and my God!" Then Jesus told him, "Because you have seen me, you have believed; blessed are those who have not seen and yet have believed."

Ellen kissed the page, closed the Bible and placed it inside the bench and closed the lid. She listened. "Have you seen me, Ellen?" That still quiet voice asked. "Have you seen me?" Oh, yes, Lord, in a million places, in your universe, in the faces of strangers and those I love. In life and through death of others, Lord, I have seen you. "There's a peace that passes understanding." She felt his smile. Yes, there is.

Chapter Twenty

Newhaven

Mabel saw Pastor Levi's car stop at Suze house. She and Suze hadn't talked but surely if anything were wrong Suze would have called, but then she and Nate had gone for a ride. A smile brought sparkle to Mabel's eyes. Nate wanted her to see Britany's farm. Such activity, she had thought, seeing the men at work cutting huge limbs off of trees that had fallen during the storm.

"What are you thinking, Nate?" She'd ask. "Are Britany and her new husband considering moving back to the farm?"

Nate beamed like a proud father. "Yes, she is, Mabel and I'm taking her husband under wing to teach him the ropes of farming."

"I'm confused. Isn't he an attorney at law?"

"Well, yes he is, Mabel, but there's weekends, aren't there." Nate rolled up the window, ready to drive back to Newhaven. "Their plans are to live in the Cape in the apartment Edward has now, but to come out weekends to oversee the renovation. You'll see, there'll come a day, I believe Edward will set up shop here on the farm and become a gentleman farmer, you know one that oversees, but doesn't work in the dirt."

"Isn't that Britany's job? I mean she seems to know a good bit about farming."

"She was her daddy's boy, all right; Tom boy. But Britany's got a bit of that girly way to her. It won't be long 'til she'll be thinking of filling the nest. Yes, sir, Britany will want a baby and right away."

Mabel kept mum her finding. Britany had used a pregnancy test a month before the wedding, and if Mabel wasn't wrong in her thinking, there would be a baby making appearance. She'd been slow in recognizing Britany was already pregnant and as she chased back time and incident, Britany had not yet chosen Edward to be her lawfully wed husband. Mabel wasn't certain Edward was the baby's daddy.

Almost, Mabel wished the girl hadn't been careless in leaving the test out in the open, but maybe that was part of the plan, too. She wasn't certain where she fit into it but since she and Suze accompanied Britany to find her wedding dress, Britany treated the two like relatives. Thinking on Britany's condition, Mabel almost didn't hear Nate when he said, "Mabel, do you think we could get married come February?" So it really was going to happen? Mabel remembered the joy she'd felt at the moment.

Finding a light jacket, she decided to walk down to see Suze. There were things Suze didn't know. Suze hugger her profusely, listening intently as Mabel explained Nate's wish to be married first of the New Year. I can't bear to think of you moving away but I'm happy for you and Nate. You are just natural together." She noticed Mabel kept glancing to where she had laid the dress she intended to wear that night. "I'm going to a dinner party in the Cape, Mabel. Do you think this dress is appropriate?"

"What's the occasion, exactly?"

"I was at the church when Christ Church called our pastor and ask for help with some program, or maybe it was advice. Pastor Levi decided to go to the Cape and check it out, he ask Miss Leah and myself if we wanted to ride there with him. I was so shocked I went." Leah gave nervous laugh, "Then I was included in an invitation from the Gates couple."

"The dress will be great, not as pretty as the one you wore to Britany's wedding, but pretty enough and I'm happy you are getting out. I'll be going so you can prepare, but do let me know how it goes."

* * * * * * * *

The ride to the Cape passed quickly as Suze found her pastor and his wife lively and welcoming in their treatment of her. It was when they arrived at the Gates home, she met their friends, introduced by Daniel Gates as Prayer warriors in long standing, Suze began to real-ize the closeness they shared. There were hugs and smiles and teasing. "How long you been up?" The one named Andrew asked Daniel. She listened to the good natured ribbing. "Long enough to help Ellen and keep her from throwing me out," he replied. But it was when they announced the one who organized the search for Walden and succeeded in his capture had arrived, she stepped back into the shadow of the staircase, desiring to observe the group together as he was introduced; and not seem forward to the others because she was not one of them.

Sitting on the stairs out of sight she listened as the man was applauded, and later as Daniel and Andrew spoke to him in a hushed voice away from the others. "Now that it's over," Andrew asked, "Can you tell us how you managed to enter into our midst? Before this episode of Walden's behavior we had not heard of you, nor mention of your name."

"I had asked leave of absence to come through this part of the country. My superiors must keep track of me, even when not on duty for my country. When they learned my intentions, I was chosen to head the search for Walden. You see he has ties to every state, he has not worked secretly behind the scenes but with boldness few possess, which had them puzzled. They had no idea he was schizophrenic, mentally unbalanced along with the use of mind altering drugs." There was a pause before he continued, "I must say this is the first encounter I've dealt with a man who thought he could fly, but I realize it was the state of his mind and one of you reminded me in the Bible, one of the Kings ate grass when he had fallen low." Suze leaned forward to listen closer, the voice made her heart race.

"You read our Bible?" Daniel's voice sounded pleased. "I'm impressed. That's great."

"It was here, in your garden, my friend, a dear friend and I listened to your sweet little daughter explain scripture." The man's voice mellowed. "A friend," I admit, who no longer believes in me due to this assignment. Your expressions ask me why, the why is because for protection I had to cover my identity."

Andrew was quick to pick up on the meaning behind the man's words. "I take it you are speaking of a lady," to which the man nodded. Andrew gave a slight chuckle. "I've run the gamut on disappointing women. In my former days I didn't care, but now that I've settled down to see the worth in my Anne, I see things differently. If the lady is someone we know, Dan and I would be happy to put in a good word for you."

"I am short on time. Walden kept us busy and while doing it made a mess of our schedule." His voice was becoming mellow as he dropped into his foreign speech. "It is with great sadness I will leave behind one I dreamed of establishing a long relationship," he sighed, "she will never know." Embarrassed, he heaved a great sigh. "Please, let us speak no longer of this nor mention again."

Suze heard them move away from the stairs. Her heart was racing and about to fly out of her chest. She gripped her hands together. How could this be? The story was too close to her own and yet she knew that was possible. According to Ellen's prayer there had been a number involved in last night's mission. Thankful for the spaciousness the Gates home offered, she kept distance from the others, until hearing soft music she wandered down the hall. It took a minute for her eyes to adjust to the girl in the room reading by one dim lighted lamp on the night stand, while soft music played nearby.

"Hello," Ruthie welcomed her from the shadows where she sat against the headboard of her bed, a book in her hand. Patting the bed, Ruthie welcomed her. "Come in, sit beside me?" Suze hesitated. "It's all right, my parents would be happy to know I have someone to talk with, too." She giggled. "Angeline and I read the boys to sleep and she is there now in case one awakens."

"Who is Angeline?" Suze was very hesitant, but Ruthie was smoothing the cover where she had moved from to make room for Suze.

"Come on, you can sit with me a minute. I feel you are a bit left out, the others are so caught up in each other because they have been friends many years and shared memories that last forever."

"You speak wisely for one so young, Ruthie. How old are you?"

"Then you remember me?" Ruthie smiled, "from the garden when we read scripture together." She continued on, "Angeline is the twin's sitter. You know we have two sets of twins. When I was small I had the most wonderful person as my sitter. Her name was Bitty because she was small. But Bitty died and we were sad. We loved her so very much."

"And do you love Angeline?"

"We do, but we've not had enough time to love her as much as I loved Bitty." Ruthie reached for Suze hand. "Angeline cannot read.

I am teaching her to read but we are using this book, The Secret Garden."

Suze stared at the book Ruthie placed in her hand. "It is about a boy neglected by his father when his mother died and his father cannot face the pain of her leaving. Then a little girl, who is a niece to the father, comes to live in the home when her parents die, but the boy's father stays away from them."

Ruthie peered up into Suze's face. "There was a lot of sadness they didn't understand." Taking the book, Ruthie continued to hold her hand. "A poor boy came along and helped them discover they must not give up, although they had lost their mothers and their father's abandoned them."

"How did he help them?" Suze asked. "Sometimes sadness can break hearts."

"He allowed them to walk in the secret garden. It had belonged to the boy's mother but when she died the father locked it up. No one was supposed to go there, but the poor boy found it." Ruthie held onto Suze hands. "Have you ever locked anything away that made you sad, Miss Suze?"

"You remember my name?"

"God helps me with these things." Ruthie glanced toward the door. "Last night I dreamed someone tried to come into our house, but our home was protected. It wasn't the security system. It was God. I thought I dreamed it, but today I heard Daddy Daniel say to Momma that Mr. Walden tried to come here last night but God protected our family." Ruthie exchanged the book for her Bible.

"I was here, last night with Miss Leah and your mother and we prayed a lot."

"I love Miss Leah. She will be happy when she has her baby." Ruthie turned on her stomach. "Let me read a passage to you…" She smiled, "Now that everything is all right in our world, we can…."

"There's our girl," Daniel's voice resounded as he switched on the ceiling light to Ruthie's room. "Oh, I'm sorry, Miss Suze, I didn't know you were here," he apologized."I wanted Ruthie to tell our guest goodbye."

Suze had risen with the surprise of additional light to the room. She and the guest of honor stood face to face, one no more surprised than the other, while Daniel Gates had no idea the ripple of emotions coming to light, nor could he understand the expression on his guests face.

"Suze Norman," he said, "Meet the man behind the capture of Clayton Walden...."

Suze whisked past the two men, without a handshake or the courtesy of a greeting. Instead, "Excuse me," she said hurrying out the room.

"Stephen Silvi," Daniel completed the introduction, looking to Ruthie for explanation. Ruthie was trying to hide a smile that erupted into laughter. "Ruthie, this is not the time for laughter. Mr. Silvi deserves respect."

"I respect Mr. Silvi," Ruthie explained. "Would you like to sit on my bed, Mr. Silvi, or there's a bench in front of my dressing table."

"That's a bit small." Daniel said, glancing from one to the other, they seemed to understand each other. A smile played about Stephen's mouth and his eyes were twinkling as he winked at Ruthie.

"I believe I've offended Miss Suze, what do you think Ruthie?" Grinning, Ruthie nodded. "I believe, Daniel, if you don't mind I will seek her out and try to become friends." Stepping forward he offered his hand to Ruthie. "What do you think? Do I have a chance Miss Suze will listen to me?"

Ruthie held his hand for a minute and then advised, "She's in the garden. That is the best place."

"Am I missing something, here?" Daniel scratched his head, wondering."Do you know, Ruthie?"

She nodded. "Is there something I should know?" Ruthie smiled. "You're not telling me? All right, then." Daniel wandered back down the hall to the gathering. His close knit friends and prayer warriors welcomed him completely unaware anything unusual happened. Through the window he saw Stephen walking toward the angel. Miss Suze was nowhere to be seen and Daniel was completely confused.

Chapter Twenty One

"You look beautiful," Stephen said, finding her, as she sat on the bench holding the Bible, "but you are sad." The Angel's wings offered protection, whether real or not, he thought. In the shadow of the angel, he was not happy to see the sadness written on her face. "Suze, I'm sorry, I mislead you."

"You were never on an island. You are not an engineer. You probably don't come from Spain and I'm not sure your mother has died, you are an expert offering your information which is completely untrue."

If he expected anger, there was only this flat voice resolved to think the worst of him.

She glanced up to see Stephen's expression displaying anger, or was it sorrow, now that she had voiced her own misgivings.

"My time in Newhaven has passed; I have tonight in the Cape. This business with Walden required more effort and time than we believed." He spoke in normal tone, plying his trade, praying to overcome her raw emotions. "I truly feel there's something good between us. You would not be upset if I meant nothing to you. I'm asking forgiveness and I hope you will give me another chance. By your rules I've been too slow in speaking my true devotion to you; I've hidden the fact my thoughts are with you every waking hour and I'm thankful for opportunity to tell you, because I cannot give you up, my lady. Now it is up to you."

Stepping inside the spreading angel wings, he sat down beside her. "May I?" He asked, taking her hand. They sit in silence listening to the ticking away of time on his watch. When she did not reply, he turned. With his finger he trailed up her cheek, gathering tears and when finished, he leaned to kiss her lips. "There's nothing more I can offer," he whispered. "I declare my love and devotion for you and offer a life for us together." Once more he waited in silence, until finally he spoke, his voice heavy with accent she had learned happened in stressful times, "You tell me nothing in return. If it is your wish I leave, then you must tell me."

Suze was fully conscious of the fact; Stephen was asking forgiveness for denying her the truth. To her surprise he spoke of love and commitment while her mind was confused, trying to understand his job required barriers of protection she was not privilege to, now or in the future. It was her time to decide was Stephen Siri worth the understanding he asked from her or would he be a stone of worry around her neck? Did she want to live the rest of her life alone remembering Wade, growing sadder day by day? "I could never forget Wade," She whispered, completely unaware she had spoken. "He was part of me, the breath I shared, part of my heart that kept us together all those years."

"If it is your love for your husband and not your anger for present circumstance," Stephen offered, "I believe we can build a love of our own, remembering kindly my wife and your husband, but as the years go by it will be our world, our life, our love and I would learn about your God. Perhaps your God allowed us to meet. Any day, lack of interest would have given us freedom to forget each other, but we did not."

For the first time, sitting beneath the angel's wings, Suze smiled. "You are willing to know my God?"

"I've had this intense desire to understand more," Stephen replied. "A man does not always ask someone to explain. I hoped in time you would help me with my questions that I might understand."

"You are so serious," Suze said, "If I bring out only that trait in you, perhaps I'm the wrong one…"

"No, no, my lady, one's God to worship and one's wife to marry that is serious business. In the short time I've known Daniel Gates and Andrew Graves; I realize they are good people. Indeed, we are guest of fine people, why don't we use the moments that follow to allow our mind to know what we should do. If it is true, your God hears our prayers, he has heard mine many days."

Ruthie and Daniel noticed their return from the garden, but it was Daniel went to them. Whether it was their countenance, Daniel was unsure; it was as if a dark cloud surrounded the two. He did not understand, nor did they for unrest hung in the air. "Is there something I can do for you?"

"No, everything is in control; we merely had business to discuss, but Mrs. Norman has not committed to the deal and possibly she is not in agreement with my proposition."

"Forgive my lack of knowledge Stephen. I simply was not aware you two knew each other."

Stephen was hesitant. "Sometimes, Daniel, one person feels they know another, but the feeling is not mutual." Turning to Suze, he said, "My lady, I believe my business here is finished. I will be going. It would be my pleasure to see you home."

"It is an hour's drive," Suze replied, truly they neither knew what to do as Ruthie came to stand with them. Taking first, Stephen's hand

and then Suze's, she said, "Do you remember when we were in the garden? I heard you say, if life could be as serene as this setting, and you praised my daddy's skill. There was a longing, do you remember? What did you long for? Whether you go on together or walk alone, praise God for this chance meeting. There will be a blessing, you may not realize it now, but later you will see God's hand working in your lives." Ruthie then fell silent as hearts began to communicate.

They could have been standing under a dome, cut off from the others, for no one listened as the world around them continued at its own pace. Daniel felt the peace of God surround them, somewhere in conversation; Ruthie had drawn him into the circle. He felt the kindness of his Savior settle, as a mantle, upon his shoulders. He recognized the scripture she was quoting, *let the peace of understanding…* The tiredness left his body as he gave thanks and he wondered what Stephen and Suze were experiencing.

So this is the fullness of prayer. *You have shone kindness upon me and the men last night and given us protection. Thank you. I want to give my life to you if you will forgive me and take me as I am with all my faults which I will work with daily under your guidance. I see Suze. If it is your will I would like to begin life with her. If it is not your will I ask you to help me understand and stay with me and fill the spot in my heart where she lives.* Stephen felt as though his mind had left his body and he was communicating, really communicating with the God he had been trying to reach these last days.

How can I leave behind Wade, whom I loved with all my heart? Is there room for another? I have such fear I cannot measure up to Stephen's expectations. Yes, you have always lived in my heart since I was a child. You say I'm unique; there is no one like me. I'm special? Joy fills my heart that you would tell me. I will praise you all the days of my life and thank you for watching over me. Yes, I will trust in you. I do praise you and thank you for always being with me. Suze communicated with her

Heavenly father as always but this time she listened. He was happy that she was unique? Joy filled her soul.

Ruthie let go their hands, smiling as she hugged each one in turn and received a kiss on her brow from Daniel as her mother joined them. "I'm sorry you both must leave early. Suze and I have become good friends over the last twenty four hours and we are blessed in meeting you, Stephen."

Suze walked outside with Stephen. She had seen God's hand directing her life, even when she failed to follow; through grief and the process of going on after Wade's death, she was never alone.

"What have you decided, my lady?" His smile was warm and trusting. Finally, his mind was at ease.

"Exactly which island do you live on?" She asked a mischievous sparkle in her eye. "A girl likes to know where she is going to live and just for my peace of mind, was any of what you told me true?"

"All was true. I was borne in Spain, educated to be an engineer which introduced me to this occupation and all I spoke of concerning my family, is truth."

"You cannot imagine the pain I felt thinking our relationship was built on lies, now I understand."

"There has never been a happier man," Stephen exclaimed as he took her into his arms. For a moment they simply stood there, savoring the comfort a human receives in the arms of one who cares. "This must be how it feels in the arms of Jesus," Stephen confided. "I ask him into my heart and I feel his presence. Tonight I am twice blessed."

The End

Epilogue

Christmas that year was one of the most blessed events the friends would remember. As usual Dan and Ellen were host to all. The Gates home was decorated for the season, red bows, holly berries, a huge tree that touched the ceiling and beautiful wreaths, but the entry held the décor most loved by all.

Even the twins with hushed voices studied the statues of Mary and Joseph and baby Jesus. In the background, three wise men appeared intent on reaching the holy one and to each side the shepherd boy and his sheep held ground as the twins gave them generous hugs and placed damp kisses on their faces. Danny and Samuel were the leaders, whispering instruction to M.J., Noel, Holly, Andy and Adeline how they could crawl around the Bethlehem group using the path they'd already established.

"That's right," Sammy encouraged, "You have to lay your candy right there at the feet of Joseph. He's a carpenter and he's hungry.

"Good boy," he said, patting Noel on the head. "Bring more, Mary's hungry."

Ruthie heard her brother and smiled. Their mother added only a few candy pieces to the bowl each day. "Don't tell on me, Ruthie," she said, "But we can't have rotten teeth in your brother's mouths." Listening to the music in the background Ruthie felt the joy in her heart expand as she saw who was coming down the sidewalk. Grandma and Grandpa, her mother's parents and for a brief moment her heart ached for one she had loved, who had been there when so badly needed, Bitty. But then the others arrived and Ruthie turned loose knowing Bitty was having Christmas with Jesus.

Miss Suze entered first, followed by Mr. Stephen carrying a bag filled with gifts, the sides bulging and reluctant to come through the door until he removed enough packages to let it bump through. There were hugs and exclamations of happiness in seeing each other again. "You're getting married, here, today," Ruthie whispered, joy causing her whisper to explode in the air. "And Mr. Nate and Mrs. Mabel are too." She danced a little dance. "You are so beautiful, Miss Suze."

Stephen stooped to kiss Ruthie's cheek. "She is beautiful, Ruthie, inside and out, I agree?"

"Wait until you meet Anne and Andrew's little girl, Adeline Grace and Marigold and Matt's Maggie. She is dressed in red." For a brief moment Ruthie remembered Marigold's baby almost didn't cry and the doctor explained to Marigold and Matt there was a problem, but when they all hugged each other, they felt the warmth claim their body, and one by one they knew little Maggie was just fine and they must remember always to say thank you when they said their prayers. Levi and Leah came carefully up the walk, by now Leah was appearing very much with child. The Gibson's, Aunt Georgia and Aunt Harriet arrived with all kinds of candies. Haley and her husband, Rosie and her son, the list went on and on as they dropped in to say

Merry Christmas and it was a day they would never forget. "We are blessed," Daniel said in welcoming all to share the day, "Our hearts are full of His love as we come together to celebrate Jesus birthday."

Thus, the vows were said that tied two hearts together; Brother Joe standing with Pastor Levi, in a room aglow with loving friends.

Candlelight gleamed from sconces on high while Christmas carols played softly, from Ellen's angel in the garden where tiny lights lined the path to the fountain that bubbled quietly in the background and the sheltering Angel bore witness to reason for the season.

"She couldn't hurt Marigold," Haley whispered to Anne. "That's why Britany and Edward aren't here."

"Don't be surprised if they arrive late," Anne replied. "Ellen can't stand to leave anyone out and since Edward is partner with Andrew," She paused, her eyes squinted as she thought on the subject. "Let's just say, my thinking is she's checked it all out with Marigold and any minute they'll come through that door."

The doorbell rang as they sit down to the table. Daniel answered and came back with Britany and Edward in tow.

"Merry Christmas, everyone."

www.ingramcontent.com/pod-product-compliance
Lightning Source LLC
Chambersburg PA
CBHW060534160726
47991CB00001B/317